THE PSALMS

Structure, Content, and Message

Claus Westermann

Translated by Ralph D. Gehrke

AUGSBURG Publishing House • Minneapolis

THE PSALMS
Structure, Content, and Message

Seventh printing

First English-language edition published 1980 by Augsburg Publishing House, Minneapolis. Translated from the second German edition published by Calver Verlag Stuttgart.

Original German edition published 1967 under the title *Der Psalter,* copyright © Calver Verlag Stuttgart. English translation copyright © 1980 Augsburg Publishing House.

Manufactured in the U.S.A.   AF 10-5300

99   98   97   10   11   12   13   14   15

Contents

Introduction

A call to praise

Bless the Lord, O my soul;
   and all that is within me, bless his holy name!
Bless the Lord, O my soul,
   and forget not all his benefits (Ps. 103:1-2).

What sort of call is this? An unknown person, with a world view, environment, and life-style infinitely distant from ours, used these words to raise a call that was primarily self-addressed. But this summons has the remarkable capacity to evoke an echo in those who hear it. It is a call to praise the holy name. It is a personal name, the personal name of a god, like that of any other god in any other of the many ancient religions which have now passed from the scene; it is the name Yahweh which is called upon in this 103rd psalm and in other psalms as well. These are psalms which belong to a religion far removed from us, and this is a call to praise a God who seems distant, too.

Nevertheless something happens when we read these words today, when we learn to follow this summons to praise a God from a distant world, when we translate it from its language into our own, and when we become accustomed to the call and speak it or sing it. We then take our place in a history which has not been interrupted since that unknown person of the people of Israel first caused the call to sound forth.

We should pause here a moment and marvel at what confronts us. What sort of call is this? It is neither a spiritual heirloom nor a leftover relic bearing witness to the tenacious power of religious rites; for this summons to praise has in fact succeeded in breaking through the limitations and boundaries characteristic of religions. Hence if a modern person hears and understands the call with which Psalm 103 begins, if that person takes it up and repeats it, then something inexplicable happens: this call is miraculously handed on, and, once begun, it can no longer be silenced.

That the call to praise has such an effect cannot be based on anything else but the foundation given in the psalm itself: ". . . and forget not all his benefits."

"Bless (or praise) the Lord . . . and forget not!" These two calls both have the same meaning. Why did this unknown person address this call to himself? So that God's benefits would not be forgotten. The coordination of "bless" and "forget not" expresses a profound truth: only those who praise do not forget. One may indeed speak about God, and still have forgotten him long ago. One may reflect upon the nature of God, and still have long since forgotten him. Forgetting God and turning away from God always begins when praise has been silenced. The secret of praise is the power it has to make connection with God; through praise one remains with God. This power of praise to make connection with God is what propels the call of Psalm 103 across the centuries and into the presence of those living today.

We live in an age whose most distinctive and perhaps important characteristic is *speed*. The tempo of today's traffic is only one example of the speed with which events of a technical, intellectual, or political nature develop—attracting us and carrying us along as individuals as well as groups. Corresponding to the pace of these developments is a great measure of *forgetting*, to a degree previously unknown in the history of the world. Because people are limited in their ability to perceive and digest sensory impressions, the only way they can deal with today's constant stream of stimuli is by forgetting most of what they experience. Those who wish to live in this age and not be continually and regretfully clinging to the past must develop a great ability to forget. For example, if people want to participate in current events by reading newspapers, they must have an ability to forget much of what they read. Yet because such a great ability to forget is unavoidable in our age, the danger is ever growing that what we lose are the vital, overarching connections which integrate our lives.

Therefore the call at the beginning of Psalm 103 takes on new meaning, placing it at the center of our life today with its problems. The call not to forget God's benefits reminds us of the one thing that integrates our lives and gives them meaning. The summons to praise God offers us participation in that which alone is steadfast, which alone can fit into a unified whole the many individual moments that change so rapidly and restlessly. This summons accomplished the same purpose for that unknown person who first uttered it long ago in a world far different from our own.

Praise of God affirms joyfully, thankfully, and with a sense of relief the great power who unites and spans the heights and depths of human existence,

... who forgives all your iniquity,
   who heals all your diseases,
who redeems your life from the Pit,
   who crowns you with steadfast love and mercy (vv. 3-4).

The Psalms embrace these great contrasts. In never-ending and yet ever-new ways they always circle about one center: human existence in its mighty, terrifying, and glorious rhythm of loss and rescue, cry for help and shout of exultation, capture and release, laughter and weeping. Even more profound and more comprehensive than such contrasts are those of being near to God and far from God. Turning away, revolting, and being indifferent to God can all be restored and healed by the one "who forgives all your iniquity."

In a mighty image that needs no further explanation, this psalm praises the mystery of the power that integrates the contrasts and disjunctions of human life. This power encompasses such tremendous dimensions that in its presence the most extreme contrasts in human existence become small and insignificant:

For as the heavens are high above the earth,
  so great is his steadfast love toward those who fear him;
as far as the east is from the west,
  so far does he remove our transgressions from us (vv. 11-12).

This image sketches the effect of God's forgiving grace in the two dimensions most extensive for people of that time. If today we want to understand what is meant, we must refer to the macro- and microcosmic dimensions revealed to us by the research of natural scientists. The God whom the Psalms praise is not the God of religious conceptualizations but the Lord of the great universe, the Commander of cosmic dimensions. This Lord is *by nature* able to give meaning and integration to both the high and low points in the lives of individuals. If we moderns are to understand what vv. 11-12 mean in our day we must repeat them when we take off in an airplane. In the midst of the plane's ascent into the clouds we must hide ourselves in the words of the psalm.

The psalm, however, points us beyond this still penultimate dimension to that which is ultimate:

For he knows our frame;
    he remembers that we are dust (v. 14).

God remembers that we are only dust. God does not forget who we are and what we are. God's great goodness transcends all dimensions and turns to these specks of dust. God considers us tiny, insignificant people worthy of forgiveness but at the same time does not forget who we are who receive this goodness: perishing human beings.

At this point the summons of the psalm first receives its basic tonality. "You infinitesimally small human, do not forget what connects your little life to the mighty dimension of eternity. Praise, praise with all your being the eternal God for sending fatherly goodness into your life; for somewhere and in some way your life participates in something which is in sharp contrast with human frailty: the steadfast love of the Lord."

But the steadfast love of the Lord
    is from everlasting to everlasting
    upon those who fear him,
    and his righteousness to children's children (v. 17).

All this should strike us more forcefully than any previous generation in view of the forces we have learned to unleash and control and the potentially rapid development of technological masters and servants, promises and threats. The praise of the eternal God, who from dimensions far beyond us pours fatherly goodness into our limited existence, is something which corresponds to the dimensions in which our generation has learned to think and move. The call not to forget is what gives meaning and direction to the chaotic structures of organization, achievement, and failure in which we live. Oh how much our age needs this! And how it secretly longs for it!

The significance of the Psalms in the Bible

Psalms, human responses to God's word and actions are heard throughout the entire Bible, from the first book to the last. The Creator's praise is heard in the account of creation; and in the book of Revelation God's final deed is followed by praise of the creation's Perfecter. Whenever God acts, there must be a response of praise. Hence praise is an essential part of the accounts of God's great deeds. The song of those who have been rescued rises up at the Reed Sea (Exodus 15); the conquest is accompanied by the song of victory (Judges 5); the barren woman whom God has comforted celebrates the reversal of her destiny (1 Samuel 2); the king celebrates the help of his God (2 Samuel 22). Apart from these psalms, which are scattered through the historical books of the Old Testament, a deep connection exists between psalms and historical accounts. Israel's earliest writing about its history grew out of its declaration of praise for God's acts of deliverance.

Yet human response to God's acts, whether by the individual or the community, consists not only of praise. Those who are smitten by God's blows, or plagued by God's silence and his turning away from them, cry out from their trouble; they pour out their hearts to God; they lament. Laments also accompany the entire path God traveled with the chosen people described in the Bible—beginning with the laments of the people in the wilderness and of Moses, the lonely mediator between God and the people, continuing with the laments of Elijah and the prophets (especially Jeremiah) and the people's laments in Babylonian exile (the book of Lamentations) and ending with Jesus' tears over the city of Jerusalem and his cry from the cross ("My God, my God, why hast thou forsaken me?" Matt. 27:46; Mark 15:34).

Praise and *lament* are the two basic melodies which, like echoes, accompany God's actions on this long path of history.

In the Psalms they are developed into mighty fugues and variations. This polarity of praise and lament is different from the familiar polarity of petition and thanksgiving in our modern prayers. The arc which the pendulum makes as it swings between the poles of lament and praise is much greater than that between petition and thanksgiving.

This is closely connected with another difference: in the Psalms singing and praying (which in later times became more and more separated) were still united; psalms are sung prayers or prayed singing. As songs they are at the same time what we call poetry. To be sure, they are poetry in a different sense than our modern poetry, but for all of that they are still formulated, "poetic" expressions of thought. Thus the Psalms still unite in themselves what for us are three separate types of compositions, which in the course of subsequent centuries have split apart. They are *prayers* (words directed to God in supplication or rejoicing), *poetry* (poetical expressions of thought), and *song* (they go beyond the mere speaking or even recital of a poem and become music).

As a unity of prayer, poetry, and song, the Psalms belong to a world which is no longer our world, and we will never fully understand or appreciate much of what is in them. But precisely because of their strangeness they speak from that distance a language which possesses validity for every age and which can be heard anew in every age. The Psalms are inexhaustible. It is an often-noted fact that in the catastrophes of the last decades the Psalms were discovered anew at many different places by many very different people. All found in them something by which our often weak and anemic praying can be renewed: an immediacy or directness of speaking to God which connects reality in all of its breadth, depth, and harshness with the God who is the Lord of both the righteous and the wicked, the God of the depths and the heights, the Lord of creation and the Lord of history.

How the Psalms originated

The answer to the question of the Psalms' origin which recent psalm research has formulated amounts to a surprising discovery, one which has had revolutionary significance for all subsequent study of the Psalms.

Until into the 19th century people had understood superscriptions at the beginning of psalms such as "A Psalm of David" to refer to authorship, and had unconsciously transferred our modern conceptions of the origins of a poem to the origins of psalms. But now a new understanding of the life and institutions of ancient Israel has forced us to adopt an entirely new viewpoint.

The Psalms did not originate as literature originates among us; rather, they arose out of the worship of Israel, as an essential component of this worship in its variety of forms. Odd as it may sound to us, the Psalms were not first written and then sung, but *vice versa*. Most of the psalms were first sung and prayed for a long time before they were written down. Those who wrote them down were not the same people who composed them; instead, they were the ones who collected them. The process of collecting and writing down the Psalms was in itself a very important and significant step, but it was a step which came somewhat late in their development. It presupposed a long, rich, and varied life of the Psalms in oral tradition.

The Psalms originated in worship. But how should we imagine that this happened? The worship in which the Psalms originated and lived was basically different from worship in our world, for worship in that culture was the natural and undisputed center of the entire community's life. Worship was not just the place where people interested in religion gathered; rather, worship was the heart in which and through which the life of all pulsated. Therefore its most important characteristic was that everything that happened in the life of the people as a whole and of individuals in particular somehow necessarily came into contact with worship and was related to worship.

A great national crisis, drought, threat of attack, defeat, or plague *had* to be brought before God in lament and supplication. Out of this grew the *community psalm of lament* (CL). If, on the other hand, victory had been granted to the nation, the land had been liberated from its enemies, threatening danger had been averted, or a bumper harvest had been received, God *had* to be praised. Out of this grew the song of thanksgiving or *community psalm of narrative praise* (CP).

The very same thing took place in the life of the individual. In this case it was both natural and necessary that the heights and depths, the anxiety and the rescue were experienced in relation to God and would therefore arouse the reactions of lament and supplication or praise. These experiences are reflected in the *individual psalm of lament* (IL) and the *individual psalm of narrative praise* (IP).

Even in the later period when the Psalms were being collected, their origin was still understood to have been in experiences of crisis and rescue. This is reflected in the superscriptions affixed to the Psalms as they were collected, e.g., to Psalm 3 ("A Psalm of David, when he fled from Absalom his son") or to Psalm 18 ("A Psalm of David the servant of the Lord, who addressed the words of this song to the Lord on the day when the Lord delivered him from the hand of all his enemies, and from the hand of Saul"). Many such examples could be cited. Even if these superscriptions were affixed to the Psalms only subsequently (in part, it seems, centuries after their origin), they are nevertheless an important witness to the fact that even in such later ages people realized that the Psalms had originated in actual life situations.

The events the Psalms speak about and out of which they arose, did not themselves take place in worship, but rather occurred in the lives of individuals or in the life of the nation. They took place in harvest fields or on battlefields, in the wilderness or in homes, on sickbeds or in the streets. Nevertheless, worship was the place where the Psalms originated. In this respect worship in ancient Israel was something different from what we understand by worship today: it was so much the center of all of life that the setting of the event from which a Psalm arose was in the vicinity of the place of worship. Often we are told of people going into the sanctuary to pour out their hearts (e.g. the mother of Samuel, 1 Samuel 1). The moving scene in Isa. 37:14-15 shows us in an especially impressive way the proximity of worship and life in those days. King Hezekiah received a letter from the enemy which in all likelihood meant Jerusalem's overthrow:

Hezekiah received the letter from the hand of the messengers, and read it; and Hezekiah went up to the house of the Lord, and spread it before the Lord. And Hezekiah prayed to the Lord. . . .

But it was not always possible to present one's prayer to God at the holy place, the sanctuary. Sick people prayed from their sickbeds, prisoners from their cells. Songs of victory arose spontaneously on the battlefield: "Hark, glad songs of victory in the tents of the righteous" (Ps. 118:15). In early Israel the holy place, the temple, was not so completely separated from the rest of the country that worship in the wider sense was possible only there. Rather, worship had its power and significance precisely because it shone forth from the sanctuary upon the entire country, all of which of course belonged to God.

Likewise the time of worship cannot be understood in terms of our modern conceptions. The great festivals, the high points of the year, were not in an exclusive sense *the* times for worship; on the contrary, as special times they were signs of the fact that time in its entirety comes from God and goes to God, and that no day in the year is without significance for worship. Prayer (calling on God and praising God) determined all existence so completely that it would have been impossible to restrict it to specific days and hours. Hence throughout the entire Old Testament we hear that festival days and ordinary days belong together; that words of thanksgiving and words of trust, words of doubt and of joy are directed to God at all times; we hear how God is summoned as witness in a quarrel or appealed to as judge, how a vow is spoken or a blessing bestowed. All of life was permeated by worship.

It is only as the temporal and spatial focus of this rich, multiform, and unrestricted worship activity in the widest sense that ancient Israel's worship at a specific place and designated time can be understood as the place where the Psalms originated. Here was the integrating and focusing center in which this entire fullness of speaking to God received its forms. Here the wide range of many thousand voices became, in an amazing manner, unison speech. This speech carried the deeply-flowing currents of many generations, and this center kept all changes in language, viewpoints, and social forms on one course. At its end this path of transmission permitted the Psalms to appear as they have been transmitted to us, still expressing themselves today in a drastically changed world.

Every individual psalm which has been transmitted to us in this book must therefore be heard out of such historical origins. Each psalm had a long and extensive prehistory. Only at the very end was it fixed in written form and included in the collection. It was first prayed, sung, and spoken by many extremely different kinds of people. Only later, at the point where these many voices were gathered in worship, did it receive the form that is normative for all and accessible to all. This process of liturgical shaping of the psalm took many generations. During those centuries each psalm was transmitted from parents to children in the collecting and focusing center of worship.

So far only psalms of praise and lament have been mentioned. Besides these there are so-called *liturgies,* i.e. psalms which permit us to recognize the combination of word and action as an event of worship (e.g. Psalm 24). A study of these liturgical psalms has not yet made possible a recovery of the "order of worship" or regulations for a festival in their entirety. The liturgical psalms are not complete liturgies; they are direct or indirect excerpts (or only reflections) of a festival. As songs or prayers of the community these psalms came to possess such an independent status in the tradition that they only hint at and do not directly present the festivals from which they come.

To say that the Psalms had their origin in Israel's worship does not mean that we must limit them to the area of the temple, to the time of established worship activity, or to the circle of Levites and sanctuary personnel. The Psalms present an essential part of the people's total life, and it was from this life that they grew.

The collection of the Psalms

It is difficult for readers or students of the Psalms to gain an overview of them because the sequence in which the 150 psalms fall is not determined by their content. One psalm follows another in what seems a random manner. This is also a result of the book's growth in various different ways over the centuries. It is impossible for us to trace the detailed steps by which the present collection came about, and that is why the result appears to be so rough and disorganized. At the beginning of the process of collection there must have been a meaningful system of organization according to content. This can be observed if one looks at the small collection in the book of Lamentations, which includes only one type of psalm.

Like our modern hymnbooks, the book of Psalms gradually grew from smaller collections. The latest organization divided it into five books (Psalms 1-41; 42-72; 73-89; 90-106; 107-150). This can be recognized by the final doxology appended to each of these divisions. (Psalm 150 is meant to be the doxology of both the final book and the entire collection.) But this division is very artificial and formal (perhaps imitating the similar division of the Pentateuch into five books), coinciding only partially with the older collections, which we can still recognize. And inside each division we can distinguish larger and smaller collections.

Larger collections. Psalms 3-41 represent a collection attributed to David. Besides their common superscription, another characteristic is that they are all psalms of an individual. Psalms 42-83, the so-called Elohistic Psalter, is recognized as a collection which once existed independently by the fact that the name *Yahweh* (Lord) is usually replaced by the name *Elohim* (God). Psalms 84-90 form an appendix to this collection. Only in Psalms 42-89 are smaller collections titled with names of guilds of singers (Asaph, Korah).

Psalms 90-106 and 107-150 were not independent collections. Between 90 and 150 there are a number of smaller collections.

Smaller collections. Within the psalms of David (3-41) still smaller subcollections are no longer recognizable. In Book II, however, Psalms 42-49 are psalms of Korah and for the most part community psalms, while 51-71 are psalms of David. At this point the growth of the collection is clearly discernible. Psalms 51-59 are laments of the individual (IL) in which the lament against the enemy is especially prominent. Several appendices were added to this closed collection: a community psalm of lament (60); four psalms of mixed genre (61-64); and as the conclusion, the psalms of praise 65-66 (66 consists of two or three psalms) together with a psalm of blessing (67). For some time the collection must have existed with this psalm of blessing as its conclusion. Later more appendices were added (68-71).

In Book III (Psalms 73-89), community psalms predominate. Almost all are attributed to guilds of singers. Most of the community laments in the Psalms are in this collection (74; 79; 80; 83; 89). If we add the fact that all the songs of Zion (46; 48; 84; 87) are psalms of Korah, it is likely that the basic collections, out of which the Psalter grew, contained psalms belonging together because of their content.

As for Books IV and V, two groups are easily and immediately discernible: the so-called enthronement psalms 93-99 (excluding 94), with Psalm 100 as the conclusion, and the psalms of praise 103-107. At one time Psalms 111-118 seem to have belonged (together with Psalms 135-136) to a collection of alleluia psalms. They were later split apart by the insertion of a closed collection, a sort of miniature psalter, the pilgrimage psalms 120-134. Psalms 119 and 137 were added as individual psalms, both having previously belonged to no particular collection. They are so different from those around them that it is very likely they were taken up individually into the Psalms as appendices. Psalm 137 is not a song for worship, but a type of folk song. Psalm 119 is also not a regular psalm, but a great edifying poem, built acrostically (on the letters of the alphabet), combining within itself almost all the types of speech represented in the Psalms.

The psalms in the little songbook made up of 120-134 each bear the superscription "A pilgrimage psalm" (that is the most likely meaning of what is often translated "A psalm of ascents"). The songs collected there are of various types. Almost all, however, are songs of the community. Only in this collection have genuine wisdom sayings been taken up (Psalms 127AB; 133). And only in this collection do we meet community psalms of praise (124; 129). The collection's concluding doxology is Psalm 134. But the brief Psalm 117 was once, it seems, thought of only as a concluding doxology to Psalms 111-116, so that Psalm 118 is in that case an appendix. But that can no longer be established with certainty.

Psalms 138-145 form a small collection of psalms of David, in the midst of which is found a group of individual laments, all uniform in form and content (140-143). At its end there is again a group of psalms of praise, the alleluia psalms 146-150.

If in the explanation of the psalms that follows we discuss psalms grouped according to content, we are actually following the collection of the psalms at an earlier stage, in which the collecting of psalms of the same type can still be recognized. Only later was this order disturbed by appendices, connections, and separations.

Superscriptions and notations

The superscriptions to the Psalms do not date to the time of their origin, but to the time when they were collected. They are something like the notes about composition or manner of singing, etc. that have been added to the beginning or end of hymns in our hymnals. These are not, of course, notes which have been added by the hymn writers themselves, but by the collectors who compiled the hymnbooks. This is the universal conviction of scholarship today, even though many of the details about these superscriptions and notations remain obscure. The only thing that is important for present-day readers of the Psalms is that this point be affirmed: *all* psalms lived in the worshiping community for a long time—usually for a very long time—without any superscriptions. Hence conclusions can be

drawn from the superscriptions only concerning the time of the
compilation and the understanding people had of the Psalms
at this stage.

Many psalms are attributed to persons or groups. Seventy-
three are attributed to David, 12 to the sons of Korah, 12 to
Asaph, 2 to Solomon, and 1 to Moses. The fact that a large
portion of the Psalms is attributed to David is entirely understandable, and is in fact based on historical tradition. Actually, however, the Psalms arose anonymously, in keeping with
their basic nature. The superscriptions arose later, at the
time when what was traditional had to be attributed to a great
personage in Israel's history. In a similar way the book of
Proverbs was attributed to King Solomon. The fact that David
was a singer and composer of songs cannot be denied. Whether
any one of the psalms attributed to him (e.g. Psalm 18) actually goes back to him is something we cannot establish.

The situation is different in the case of the psalms attributed
to the guilds of singers. The names of these guilds are mentioned in the Chronicler's history. It was their duty to foster
and pass on temple songs. It is entirely likely that specific
groups of psalms were part of the tradition of specific guilds.
However, we can no longer tell to what extent these temple
singers actually adopted older and even very old psalms.

Certain designations of the Psalms are clear, e.g. "psalm,"
"song," "song of praise," "prayer," and "song of instruction."
However, we do not always know why some designations have
been added to specific collections of psalms. The expressions
miktam (Psalms 16; 56-60; translated "a golden jewel" by Luther) and *shiggaion* (Psalm 7; translated by Luther as "innocence") have not been adequately explained.

Musical designations. The most common musical expression,
lamnassēah (usually translated as "to the choirmaster"), has
not been adequately explained. It could mean "by the out-

standing one." It is even translated by one scholar as "for the purpose of obtaining mercy." The expression often found at the end of a verse, *sĕlāh*, points toward an interlude—a responsory sung by the choir, which at this point sang the words found in Ps. 136:1 ("O give thanks to the Lord, for he is good, for his steadfast love endures forever"). The notations at the beginning of Psalms 6; 22; 46; 56 are perhaps meant to be indications of a melody. But that, as well as the individual details, is very uncertain.

But even if it is recognized that all these notations arose at the time when the Psalms were collected, the fact that we can no longer determine their original meaning does not mean our understanding of an individual psalm itself is thereby diminished. In the case of a very few psalms we learn of the use to which they were put: in connection with the dedication of the temple (Psalm 30), the Sabbath (92), and a thank-offering (100). Many of these designations are not clear ("for the memorial offering"? Pss. 38:1; 70:1); others indicate a liturgical use of the psalm in a very late period. Only in one case does the superscription completely agree with the content of a psalm. Psalm 102 is designated, "A prayer of one afflicted, when he is faint and pours out his complaint before the Lord."

The poetic form of the Psalms

It was Herder (*Concerning the Spirit of Hebrew Poetry,* 1782) who discovered the poetic form in the Psalms—something which had remained hidden because of the leveling view of Scripture as doctrine. Soon thereafter the basic characteristic of Hebrew poetry was discovered: sentence rhythm, usually called *parallelismus membrorum* (parallelism of members). This rhythmic pattern can be compared to the runners of a rocking chair. Two sentences are lined up parallel to one another. They are similar to each other, complement one another, or contrast one with the other. These three kinds of parallelism are called (a) *synonymous,* (b) *synthetic,* and (c) *antithetic.*

>   (a) Ps. 103:1
>   "Bless the Lord, O my soul;
>   and all that is within me, bless his holy name!"
>   (b) Ps. 103:2
>   "Bless the Lord, O my soul,
>   and forget not all his benefits. . . ."
>   (c) Prov. 21:26
>   "All day long the wicked covets,
>   but the righteous gives and does not hold back."

These are only the most important forms of the rhythmic pattern. Verses occur which place three phrases parallel to each other (to say nothing of still other types of parallelism). An especially artistic example is seen in Psalm 93, in which a climax is expressed by continued repetition of one part of each line:

The floods have lifted up, O Lord,
the floods have lifted up their voice,
the floods lift up their roaring (v. 3).

The statements which develop a rhythm as they are spoken, are themselves rhythmically constructed. This is not a matter of meter (number and length of syllables); there is no metrical pattern imposed from without, as in Latin or Greek poetry. Rather this rhythm arises from the nature of each individual sentence. For instance, two parallel sentences may have three beats each; this is often the case. In examples a and b above, three such beats can be recognized even in translation: "*Bless* the *Lord,* O my *soul.* . . ." The second half of the verse in Hebrew also has three beats, even though the translation does not express this as clearly. There are two other kinds of rhythms with equal beats: 2:2 and 4:4. An example of 2:2 rhythm is Ps. 113:5-6:

. . . who is *seated* on *high,* who *looks* far *down.* . . .

An example of 4:4 rhythm is Ps. 103:10:

Not according to our *sin* does he *deal* with *us,*
   nor as *fits* our *crimes* does he *punish us.*

Unequal rhythms (3:2 or 4:3) also occur, as do those with three parallel phrases of equal rhythm: 2:2:2 and 3:3:3. The lament has a peculiar 3:2 rhythm; for example, Amos 5:2:

*Fal*len, no *more* to *rise,*
   is the *virgin Is*rael.

This rhythm of two parallel statements (as well as the rhythm inside each statement) frequently varies many times in one psalm. A psalm is hardly ever built up on one identical rhythmic pattern (e.g. 3:3 from beginning to end). This corresponds, of course, to living speech, which, as words articulated in rhythm, does not permit itself to be pressed into a straitjacket. Thus this form of poetry is not so far from ordinary speech; its rhythm is not artificial, but natural. The material may move back and forth between prose and poetry. Sometimes a narrative can cross over into rhythmic form (cf. Gen. 3:14ff.); sometimes several phrases or sentences in a poem can be prose.

It is a feature of the Hebrew language (as well as of the neighboring Semitic languages) that *sentences* rather than words or syllables are rhymed. The rhyme occurs neither in sound nor in the number of words but in the *meaning* of the sentences. In this feature the ancient idea is kept alive that all human speech consists not of words, but sentences. Not the single word but the sentence as a whole is the basic unit of human speech. It is from this perspective that sentence rhythm (sentence-rhyme) or parallelism is to be understood.

Types and genres of psalms

Lament and *praise* are the two dominant tonalities that characterize the Psalms of Israel. Even though worship was the "life situation" *(Sitz im Leben)* where the psalms were used, and out of which they arose, the laments are still genuine human laments, and the praise is the joy of actual people—the joyful response to God's great acts in all its breadth and fullness. Even in festival liturgies and wisdom psalms the words are primarily those of persons—directed by an "I" to a "thou." They are only secondarily sacred words which, by being recited, represent a sacred happening or event.

Thus in the Psalms is reflected the life of the individual and of the people in all its diversity. They reflect life with its depths and heights, life lived in manifold environments between the sea and the mountains, life lived in common with trees, animals, and fields, life lived in the context of the vast history which extends from creation to God's advent to judge the world. Within such broad perspectives the life of the individual has, in the Psalms, an equally important place. The Psalms reflect the individual's joys and sorrows between birth and death, including toil and celebration, sleeping and waking, sickness and recovery, failure, anxiety, and trust, temptation to despair, and comforts received. The Psalms even reflect the grievous problem life presents when the righteous must live in the midst of evildoers, into whose hands they have been delivered.

And just as life in its fullness is articulated in various experiences, so likewise the Psalms participate in the ordered variety of all that lives. In the Psalms, forms or genres can be recognized which have the capacity to sort that variety into categories. Just as various species can be discerned in living creation (species which never can be reduced to abstract and dead classifications, but which permit each individual member to retain its uniqueness), likewise the individual psalms belong to forms or genres which permit an unlimited number of unique individual expressions.

The basic rhythm which determines all human existence, the rhythm of joy and sorrow, characterizes the two most important and most clearly discernible classes or genres of psalms: psalms of lament (L) and psalms of praise (P). But it must be added immediately that in the world of the Psalms joy and sorrow are not in the first instance human emotions which are subsequently brought into relation to God. They exist *as such* in relation to God, coming from God, living in God's presence, and going on the path toward God. Praise is joy spoken to God; lament is sorrow poured out to God. Psalms of praise and psalms of lament are both in turn classified into those of the individual (I) and those of the community (C). This differentiation follows necessarily from human existence which is always made up of both individual existence and existence with others.

Here then are the main types of psalms, listed with an example of each type:

CL	*community psalm of lament*	Psalm 80
IL	*individual psalm of lament*	Psalm 13
CP	*community psalm of narrative praise*	Psalm 124
IP	*individual psalm of narrative praise*	Psalm 30
H	psalm of descriptive praise *(hymn)*	Psalm 113

In this classification two types of psalms of praise are differentiated: psalms of narrative praise and psalms of descriptive praise. Psalms of narrative praise are usually called "psalms of thanksgiving." But our word *thank,* which has no corresponding word in the language of the psalms, cannot really express what is meant in these psalms. (The Hebrew word often translated as "thank" means "praise" or "confess"; instead of "narrative praise" one could say "confessing praise.") Yet the difference between the two types of psalms of praise is easy to understand and recognize. *Narrative* or *confessing praise* is the echo of a specific act of God which has just taken place. It is the liberated, rejoicing sigh of relief by a person who was rescued, who now says "thank God" for that rescue. Its basic structure is always "God has acted!" An especially noteworthy example of narrative praise by an individual (IP) is the collection of four songs of praise (now combined in Ps. 107:1-32) by persons who had been rescued from trouble at sea, sickness, prison, and from being lost. As narrative praise by the community (CP) I mention the "Song of Miriam" in Exod. 15:1 (Exod. 15:21), probably the oldest psalm in Israel. There are also two examples of this genre in the Psalter: 124 and 129. The remarkable fact that this group occurs so rarely will be explained later.

Psalms of descriptive praise or *hymns* (H) are not the result of one single deed of God; rather, they praise God in the fullness of his existence and activity. Their basic structure therefore is "God is . . . God does. . . ." It would be possible to distinguish between psalms of descriptive praise by an individual (e.g. Psalm 103 or 139) and by the community, but in this case the distinction is not important. As a genre the psalms of descriptive praise are songs of the community.

The main genres have now been named. Each may in turn be subdivided, for the most part in such a way that one of the motifs or elements of the genre dominates the psalm, or one of the motifs becomes an independent psalm. This is especially obvious in the case of the descriptive psalm of praise: the praise of God's majesty divides into the praise of the Creator and the praise of the Lord of history. These two motifs can become independent, as in the praise of the Creator in Psalm 8 or the praise of the Lord of history in Psalm 105. The praise of God's goodness also can dominate an entire psalm, as in Psalm 103. Or the introduction of the psalm of descriptive praise, the imperative call to praise, can become an independent psalm, as in Psalms 147 and 150. The community psalm of narrative praise can take the special form of the song of victory (Judges 5); in the case of the individual psalm of lament, the section about enemies can become dominant (Psalms 14; 52; 53); or the expression of confidence can become a distinct type of psalm, a psalm of trust (Psalm 23). Psalm 46, a song of Zion, is similar to the community psalm of trust.

In the case of many psalms a clear-cut categorization into one of these genres is impossible because they are composites of mixed genres. We know from the Chronicler's history that in the later period the boundaries between the various types of Psalms became fluid. Form became unimportant or receded into the background as living contact between all areas of life and worship decreased and temple worship became a world unto itself—an area closed in on itself, firmly shut to the outside. Hence we find in the books of Chronicles songs which are composites of entirely different psalm genres (e.g. 1 Chron. 16:8-36 is composed of parts of Psalms 105; 96; 106). From this we can conclude that the psalms of mixed genre belong to a later period.

In addition to the main types just presented, two important types of psalms still come into consideration: liturgies and wisdom psalms. As has been explained above (p. 16), these are not liturgies in the strict sense that we use the term today. Here we designate as *liturgies* all those psalms in which we can recognize a combination of liturgical action and speech, e.g. Psalm 24. Recent psalm research has laid great stress on the search for the liturgical or worship activities reflected in the Psalms. As an assured result of such research it has been established that much more about Israel's worship services, festivals, and cultic activities can be seen in the Psalms than had been noticed earlier. At the same time it has also become clear that much in the Psalms points to an extra-Israelite origin of Israel's cultic activities. But as for details, this research has produced results which are still very uncertain. Even when some researchers have assigned a great number or even the majority of the extant psalms to one single festival, no greater clarity has thereby been achieved. The cultic interpretation of individual psalms has varied so much in its results (e.g. in the case of Psalms 50 and 73) that almost everything here is still uncertain. Therefore we will designate as liturgies only those psalms in which liturgical activity is unambiguously seen to be connected with liturgical speech.

Finally, *wisdom psalms* represent an especially unique group, a transitional type between the psalm and wisdom teaching. Typical of this genre is Psalm 37. In this psalm, as in many others, the world of the Psalms and the world of wisdom meet in the great theme of the contrast of the righteous and the wicked. But we observe the transition from prayer to a sort of pious meditation (much like a wise person's reflection) also in other connections. Psalm 1 provides the entire book of Psalms with something like a prologue expressing this combination of piety and wisdom.

We have now considered the most important types of psalms. Many smaller groups can also be mentioned, e.g. royal psalms (which, however, do not represent a genuinely independent genre). By beginning with the types which have been presented here it will be easy for all who study the Psalms to find their way in the midst of the apparently unorganized arrangement of the psalms. At the same time, by means of this approach, the first and most important step toward interpreting the Psalms has been taken. An individual psalm can be adequately understood only in the context of the group to which it belongs, i.e. by comparing it with psalms of the same genre.

1

The Community Psalm of Lament (CL)

The texts

Not many psalms of this genre have been preserved in the Psalter: 44; (60); 74; 79; 80; 83; 89. Motifs or reminiscences of the CL psalm are found in Psalms 82; 85; 68; 90; 106; 115. The small book of Lamentations includes (except for chap. 3, an IL psalm) only CL psalms, although only chap. 5 presents a pure form, while in chaps. 1, 2, and 4 CL motifs have been combined with those of the lament for the dead.

In the prophetic books we sometimes find complete examples of the CL genre (Jeremiah 14; Isa. 63:7—64:12; Habakkuk 1), sometimes parts or motifs from them (Isaiah 26; 33; 51; 59; Joel 1-2; Jeremiah 3). In many ways Deutero-Isaiah's proclamation of salvation reflects the laments of the people in exile (e.g. Isa. 40:27). The situations from which psalms of lament arise are referred to many times throughout the entire Old Testament. Sometimes, as in Joel 1-2, the ritual enactment of a lament is described at length; more often it is expressed only in a statement, e.g. "Then the children of Israel cried to the Lord . . ." (see Judg. 20:23-26; 21:2-4; 1 Kings 8:33ff.; Isa.

15:2-4; 58:3-5; Jer. 36:6-9; Hos. 7:14). The people's cry to the Lord in the wilderness belongs here, so that the first beginnings or forerunners of the CL genre must reach back into the time of Israel's wanderings in the wilderness.

The liturgical action

What took place whenever such lamentation was raised by the people is known very precisely from the many texts mentioned above and also from many others. In fact, no worship observance in ancient Israel is as well known to us as is the special rite of lamentation, often called a "fast" *(sôm)*. Since it was always precipitated by a special crisis, fasting had to be announced in preparation for the rite. The community had to be called together for it, and that meant the entire people, including women and children (cf. the summons to community laments in Ezek. 21:12; Joel 2:16; Jonah 3:5). Part of the observance of a fast included the purification of the worshipers (Joel 1:14), abstinence, and garments of mourning. Above all, girding on sackcloth (Isa. 22:12; Jer. 4:8; 6:26), sprinkling one's head with dust and ashes (Josh. 7:6; Neh. 9:1), gestures of humiliation and entreaty, and "weeping before the Lord" (Judg. 20:23-26; Jer. 14:12) were part of this observance, as were the community psalms of lament.

There once existed in Israel many more psalms of lament than those which have been passed on to us. It is clear, even if one counts only the number of excerpts from psalms of lament which are quoted in Deutero-Isaiah, that many more once existed than have been preserved in the Psalms. No Israelite ever lived who had never heard the sound and words of these gloomy psalms of lament, and who could not associate with them special and unforgettable hours and days. The special thing about these days of fasting and lament was that they did not occur regularly. They were not on any liturgical calendar. Rather they were observed spontaneously whenever a crisis sent out the call: a drought perhaps, or a plague of grasshoppers, an enemy attack or a distastrous defeat, the destruction of a city or a sanctuary. Hence these community laments were intimately connected with such difficult experiences for the people, a city, or a region.

If our book of Psalms contains so few community psalms of lament (many fewer than is in keeping with their importance), this is because the Psalter is a collection from the late period when Israel was a mere province inside an empire, when the temple community stood at a remote distance from the events which in earlier days had always given rise to the special rite of lamentation. The place of the old liturgical observances of lament had been taken over by the service of penitence, such as the one described programmatically in Ezra 9. The prayer transmitted there exemplifies the transition from the psalm of lament to the prayer of repentance.

An example: Psalm 80

Verses 1-3. Psalm 80 begins with the introductory petition attached to the address. The passionate pleading in the extended address, combined with elements of the praise of God, is akin to the invocation of the deity whom ancient songs of victory invoked. The basic tone of these sturdy songs is first heard in the cry to God from most desperate need. God is attested as the one who, enthroned above the cherubim, came to aid the people, causing the very earth to shake. "Stir up thy might . . ." the hard-pressed people pleaded, because they recalled God's great deeds in the past. Verses 8-11, which unfold these deeds of yore, can be linked directly to an invocation, "Were you not the one who . . . ?"

The many verbs of the imploring petition in vv. 1-3 permit us to recognize the bipartite form of all petitions in the Psalms: the living God can be appealed to for aid only by first of all being asked to turn, appear, hear, and cause his countenance to shine forth. God is neither a rescue machine nor a supernatural force. God is a person, and one can ask him for help only when that personhood is taken seriously.

Verses 4-7. After the introductory petition comes the complaint. (The German noun *Klage* can be translated as "lament" or "complaint." When used to refer to a psalm genre, we have translated it as "lament" (Community Psalm of Lament). When it is used to refer to one of the elements in the psalm of lament, it is translated as "complaint.") It begins at the point where the trouble had its origin: with God's relationship to the suppliant (v. 4 has been poorly preserved; perhaps we are to read, "O Lord God of hosts, how long wilt thou be angry [and keep silent while thy people pleads with thee?"]). Whatever is tormenting the people and driving them on toward death ("how long . . . ?") is something that can be traced back to God. That which has come upon those who lament began there. Every statement from vv. 4b-6a begins: thou . . . thou . . . thou! The complaint directed toward God—the accusation of God—is the nerve center of all lamentation in the Psalms. Every lament somewhere strikes at the one who as Creator and Lord allows suffering to come upon his creatures. The laments of the Old Testament search for the cause of suffering not in some power hostile to God but in God alone. The accusation against God combines with the complaint about the person's own suffering in the powerful images of the bread of tears and the cup of tears. Even eating and drinking are no longer refreshment and strengthening, but part of the misery. (This is stated even more strongly in Lam. 3:15-16.)

In verse 6 the third element of the complaint is added: a look at enemies and their mockery. This is continued in vv. 12-13, again in combination with the accusation against God.

In verse 7 the complaint flows into the petition which recurs as a refrain through the entire psalm (vv. 3, 7, 19). Reflecting the artistry of the psalmist, this refrain occurs only where a petition fits in with the sense; it is not used mechanically at the end of each strophe.

Verses 8-11. Completely in keeping with the accusation against God is the review of God's past saving acts, which stand in such stark contrast to God's present actions. The complaint chides God for this contrast. Yet, despite everything in this chiding the one who complains still clings to past personal experiences of God's goodness and faithfulness. This psalm speaks of God's saving acts on Israel's behalf through the metaphor of a vinedresser, an image so richly developed in the Bible. This metaphor has no esthetic function here nor does it serve to make the point clear. Rather, as a metaphor it implies that God's dealings with his people are a *totality*—what we mean by the comprehensive term "a history." They are a totality which existed prior to the individual events and in which these events have meaning only as members of the whole. If one looks closely at the individual parts of the metaphor, one realizes that statement by statement it is unfolding the historical creed—the basic confession of faith of the people of Israel concerning the acts of God that formed the basis of their history: (a) the leading out of Egypt, and (b) the leading into the land and the growth that took place there (cf. Exod. 3:7-8). The growth of this vine in the land in which it was planted is pictured with such exaggeration that the limits of the image are almost burst. Such exaggeration in a creed is meant as a marveling, amazed reference to the greatness of God's activity. The effect of the contrast is therefore added: Wilt thou consign what has grown so wonderfully and luxuriantly to complete destruction? Thus the last statement of this section already points beyond itself to a continuation of the complaint.

Verses 12-13. Earlier (v. 4) the complaint asked the question, How long? Now the corresponding question follows: Why? The metaphor permits at this point a frighteningly bold accusation of God, who is accused of participating in the destruction of the vineyard he personally planted. But this is not a mere assertion of fact; it is really the lamenter's passionate clinging to the God who is incomprehensible. In verse 13 the enemy comes to the fore. This is also stated with amazing skill by a continued use of the same metaphor: robbers plunder and destroy, and the victims can do nothing but cry to God, from whom all this has come. The sequence of v. 14 following vv. 12-13 is the same as when v. 7 (the same statement) followed vv. 4-6.

Verses 14-15. Here the two parts of the petition can again be recognized: the request to "turn again" presupposes that God has turned away in anger. Only if God turns again toward the people can they expect salvation.

Verses 16-17. The petition is connected with a wish, a double wish aimed in two directions. What is called for is God's intervention in the midst of a specific political situation in which two opponents confront one another. God's intervention *for* the one can only be understood as an intervention *against* the other. But the emphasis is on the positive. The hope is for life to become meaningful again, for God to turn again toward those who owe their lives and growth and maturity to him alone.

Verses 18-19. The conclusion of the psalm is a vow to remain faithful to God, combined with one more statement of the petition. It would be entirely misunderstood if thought of as a bargain promising God a recompense for the requested deliverance. Like every genuine vow, it is a pledge of allegiance freely made by a person who calls out of trouble to God, calling out to the Deliverer and promising loyalty beyond the hour of deliverance.

The structure of the community lament

This type of psalm begins with a call to God, which is often combined with an introductory petition for help. Then complaint follows in three parts: accusation against God, we-complaint, and complaint about enemies. These occur not in an inflexible sequence but in various interrelationships. The goal of the complaint is the petition. Usually, however, there stands between the complaint and the petition a section which turns to God's gracious acts, either in a confession of confidence or in a review of God's earlier saving acts on behalf of his people (as in Psalm 80). Then the petition comes, first of all always as a request for God to turn toward the suppliant, and then as a petition for aid and intervention. Often a third element is added: a petition against the enemy. In many psalms the petition is supplemented by reasons placed before God to support it.

At this point (after the call to God, complaint, and petition) a break occurs. Here the people (in earlier ages, at least) waited for an answer. They waited for God's oracle, which was given through someone who spoke in God's name. The divine oracle is suggested in many CL psalms, but does not actually occur in any that have been preserved in the Psalter. (We learn more about these divine oracles from the CL in the prophetic books.) These psalms end with either the petition or a vow to praise (as in Psalm 80).

This describes the essential elements of the CL structure; however, each individual psalm is an entirely unique, unrepeatable composition. Each must be heard for itself and interpreted by itself, as we have tried to do by way of example with Psalm 80. Because that is not possible in this present study, the individual parts will now be discussed in a survey of all the psalms of this genre.

The address. The address or call to God in the psalms has a greater significance or meaning than we moderns can clearly see in it. Calling upon a person by name is the necessary presupposition of calling on God. By means of the address, contact is established which makes speaking to God possible. The address is something like opening a door. If a person calls upon God by his name—or vice versa—something happens at that moment. The address is an event which unites the one who calls with the one who is called. This calling upon God is protected from misuse by the Second Commandment.

Most often God is called on by name only, without any further attributes being added: e.g. Ps. 79:1, "O God, the heathen have come into thy inheritance . . ." (so also 74:1; 83:1; 44:1; Lam. 5:1). In this very simple and completely direct calling on God the immediacy of speaking to God in the biblical psalms is apparent—standing in stark contrast to the Babylonian and Egyptian psalms, in which the address to God is almost always expanded by a fullness of doxological predicates. Such an expansion of the address is found in the Old Testament only in very late psalms (106:1-3). It occurs often in the psalms in the Apocrypha (Sir. 36:1; Song of the Three Young Men) 1:3-5; and Pseudepigrapha (Pss. Sol. 5:1-2a; 17:1-4). To a certain extent, this difference can be compared to the difference between personal and official ways of addressing people. An address which employs a person's title always presupposes a certain distance or an official, formal situation; we speak of a "stiff" relationship. An address which employs a person's personal name presupposes a closer relationship.

The complaint can follow the address immediately, as in the example cited above (79:1), but it can also, as in Psalm 80, be combined with an introductory petition, an introductory call for help: Lam. 5:1, "Remember, O Lord, what has befallen us, behold, and see our disgrace!" (So also 74:2-3; 80:1b-3; 83:1b; 106:4-5; 60:1b). It is striking that with this introductory call for help (also found in the IL), in many psalms the petition has two distinct places, before the complaint and after it.

Perhaps these were in earliest times two entirely different forms which gradually coalesced.

The complaint. The complaint is something much more lively, much more positive than what we think of today when we use the word. For us, a complaint is no longer a part of prayer. We think of complaints primarily from purely human conversations, and in this context the word always has a negative connotation. We are, in fact, sometimes surprised when a person does not complain, especially in a situation where complaining would be expected. Hence we can no longer understand what the complaint once meant in speech directed toward God. It will help our understanding if we think of the legal world, where the complaint (the accusation or indictment) still has a necessary and positive function.

The complaint in the Psalms shows its difference from our understanding in that it is always addressed in three directions. It is (1) a complaint directed against God (a "you" complaint); (2) a complaint about one's own suffering (an "I" or "we" complaint); and (3) a complaint about the acts of enemies (a "they" complaint). These three elements of the complaint stand in lively, multifaceted relationship to one another. Not all need appear in each psalm, but in its basic nature every complaint possesses these three aspects and is pointed in these directions. The complaining and lamentation in them is not done by an individual as such, nor yet by the people as a sovereign political entity, but by the human person, in the three basic relationships which comprise all human existence: self-existence, existence together with others, and existence over against God. These three aspects of the complaint permit unlimited variety, where a one-sided complaint almost always has a monotonous effect. A psalm of lament can receive its special character when one of these three aspects becomes prominent; e.g. the complaint against God in Psalm 89, the we-complaint in Lamentations 5, or the lament against enemies in Psalm 83.

The *complaint or accusation against God* can take the form of a question (Why? How long? Ps. 80:4-12) or of a statement ("Thou hast breached all his walls" Ps. 89:40). Behind the question "Why?" stands the human reaction "I (or we) cannot understand it." Behind the question "How long?" stands the assertion "I can't hold out any longer." These are questions about the meaning and goal of life. In the accusation against God, both of these questions are put to God. This means those who prayed these psalms did not doubt that God existed somewhere beyond the limit of human possibilities. Rather, God was *presupposed* as existing there. If in a borderline situation a person asked questions about life's meaning and goal, then this was questioning *directed to God*. It could not be otherwise. That the possibility of raising an accusing finger existed and questions of "Why?" and "How long?" could be raised pointed to the reality of God. We are frightened by the sharpness of these accusations:

Thou hast renounced the covenant with thy servant;
   thou hast defiled his crown in the dust (Ps. 89:39).

And to these statements many others could be added. Nevertheless such accusations are a sign that those who spoke them took their God seriously. Later on, when people could no longer understand God because of the realities they had to face, they turned their backs on him.

The *we-complaint* consists of two parts: a complaint about the trouble ("In the dust of the streets lie the young and the old" Lam. 2:21) and the shame caused by the trouble ("We have become a taunt to our neighbors" Ps. 79:4). These two sides of the we-complaint point to something important: suffering—whether that of an individual, city, or nation—is perceived as an event that always happens in the context of community.

The *accusation against the enemy* is especially elaborate in Psalms 74; 79; 80; 83. In Psalm 80 the complaint is clothed in the image of wild beasts who destroy the vineyard. This aspect must, of course, be completely absent in the laments which are raised at the time of a natural catastrophe, drought, or plague of grasshoppers. It is a striking fact that only such community laments were taken up into the Psalms which presuppose hostile action by enemies, while laments raised because of catastrophes in nature have been transmitted to us only in historical and prophetic texts (e.g. Jeremiah 14:15; Joel 1-2).

Review of God's past acts. This part of the community psalm of lament above all others exhibits the scope and breadth of the Psalms' address of God. In contrast to the community's present disturbed reality, which forces it to cry out to God, it now holds up before God what God once did for the people in times past. In language which is literarily unique, beautiful, and sturdy, Psalm 80 summarizes God's dealings with the people by means of a parable concerning the work of a gardener or vinedresser: "Thou didst bring a vine out of Egypt; thou didst . . . plant it" (v. 8). In Psalm 44 the contrast between then and now is sharp and grating:

We have heard with our ears, O God,
    our fathers have told us,
what deeds thou didst perform in their days,
    in the days of old . . . (v. 1).
Thou hast sold thy people for a trifle,
    demanding no high price for them.
Thou hast made us the taunt of our neighbors;
    the derision and scorn of those about us (vv. 12-13).

There is a similar review of God's past help in Ps. 85:1-3 and Isa. 63:11-14; it is alluded to in Ps. 83:9-11; it is changed to an extensive historical account in Ps. 106:7-46; it culminates in the promise to David in Ps. 89:19-37. The scope of such a review of God's past dealings can be opened even wider. God can be reminded of his acts of creation, of his battle against chaos at the beginning (Ps. 74:12-17; Isa. 51:9-16). When God is thus reminded of this earlier activity, and when the contrast between the past and present is placed before him, what becomes noticeable is the awakening of a sense of history. Under the pressure of the crisis this causes the persons involved to perceive two things. First, as they behold the contrast between the past and the present, they begin to see similar integrating coherences in their own history, even at the point of rupture which exposes the stark contrast they currently experience. Second, they become aware of the fact that the totality of their history rests in the acts of God alone, who heals the ruptures.

In the place of such a reminder to God of past deeds there can be a confession of confidence (Jer. 14:9-22; Ps. 115:3, 9-11; Isa. 63:16) or general praise of God (Lam. 5:19; Pss. Sol. 5:9-11). By clinging to God's gracious activity in the past, despite present trouble, the power which kept Israel alive after it had broken to pieces politically became effective. Here we can note how the praise of God's great deeds reached into the midst of the community's lament. Despite the accusation against God, the suppliants held fast to what was certain: the reality of God's trustworthiness which they had experienced in their own history.

The petition. The petition or request in the Psalms is also essentially different from what we understand by the term. It is more like what we call "entreaty." In our present word *petition* two originally different phenomena are combined: (1) the entreaty prompted by trouble (which always in some way is entreaty for deliverance), and (2) asking for something (which presupposes a need, but not acute trouble). This second element, asking for something, occurs only peripherally in the Psalms, if at all. Almost always the petitions of the Psalms are concerned with deliverance from acute trouble. We never meet what is so common and entirely natural in our modern prayers: a heaping up of individual requests. Even when a petition includes a number of sentences, it aims at only one thing: deliverance from the trouble which has been presented to God in the complaint. The petition arises from the complaint; it is the goal of the complaint.

The other essential mark of a petition has already been mentioned in connection with the initial petition in Psalm 80. The petitions in the Psalms characteristically consist of two parts. First there is a request for God's attention (Come! Arise! Consider! Hear! Behold! Be not silent! Remember! etc.). Only then does the request for God's intervention come (Help us! Free! Protect! Vindicate me! Sustain! Rescue!). These two sides occur again in the account of the one who has been delivered: "Thou hast heard. . . . Thou hast freed. . . ." Throughout the Old Testament God's helping and rescuing always has these two sides. They indicate something essential about the Israelite's relationship to God: The Israelite knew that help could come only through an encounter with the living God. Without God's personal turning toward the person in trouble, there could be no help.

Often the petition is linked to reasons, which are to strengthen it and give it emphasis. Such reasons can refer to God, ". . . for the glory of thy name" (Ps. 79:9); to enemies, "Why should the nations say, 'Where is their God?' " (Ps. 79:10; cf. 74:10, 18, 22-23), or to the petitioners themselves: ". . . we have had more than enough of contempt" (Ps. 123:3-4) and ". . . for we are brought very low" (Ps. 79:8).

Including such supporting reasons in prayers in an effort to influence God (also in the IL psalms) appears questionable to us. It seems as if God is being addressed too much like a human being. From our perspective this kind of speech is certainly a very childlike and naive way to talk to God. An espe-

cially characteristic example is the intercession of the prophet
Amos for his people: "O Lord God, forgive, I beseech thee!
How can Jacob stand? He is so small!" (Amos 7:2, 5). But we
dare not judge by our standards. And in any case this is a way
of speaking which is close to God and which expects something
from him.

The divine response. What the congregation wanted to say
when it came before God with its lament had been fully said
after it had brought its petition. But the liturgical rite, the
observance of lamentation or of fasting, was not thereby completed. First the most important thing had to occur: God's
answer. The people had come together for the purpose of
bringing their trouble before God so that he might reverse it.
At this point, after the petition, the suppliant congregation
expected that God would in some way be heard. This is exactly
what is described in Psalm 85. Verses 4-7 contain the petition,
"Restore us again, O God of our salvation. . . ." The congregation's prayer continues to this point. At verse 8, however, an
individual voice begins,

Let me hear what God the Lord will speak,
   for he will speak peace to his people. . . .

This is apparently a late, reworked description; but it shows
the original procedure. The people who had assembled for
lament actually expected God to respond to their pleading;
and this response could be heard through a servant of God,
a priest, or a prophet, and then proclaimed to those who waited
for it. In another, very late passage (2 Chron. 20:3-17), the
emergence of such an oracle of salvation is described in detail.
In this case a Levite announced the word of salvation to the
congregation (vv. 14-15). It is clear from a series of passages
in the prophetic books (esp. Amos 7-8; Jeremiah 14-15) that
the prophets, who also held the office of intercessor, often
spoke oracles of salvation at such rites of lamentation. This

was also the special office of the cult prophets (the salvation prophets), whom we know almost entirely as opponents of the canonical prophets. At this point prophecy and worship met.

In the Psalms the oracle of salvation is only rarely preserved or referred to (Pss. 60:6-8; 81:6; 85:8ff.); however, we meet it often in prophetic texts (Isa. 33:10-13; 49:22; 59:15b; Jer. 4:1-2; 51:36; Hos. 6:5-9; Joel 21ff.; Mic. 7:11-13; Hab. 3:3-15). In two of these texts, however, God's answer is no, an unconditional refusal to intervene with aid (Amos 7:8; 8:2; Jer. 14:10; 15:1-4). These two passages show that God's response to the people's plea had not been determined beforehand, but really was open. The psalms of lament presuppose this other possibility in the question with which they lament: God, why are you silent? (Hab. 1:13b); How long will you not hear? (Hab. 1:2); "Thou hast wrapped thyself with a cloud so that no prayer can pass through" (Lam. 3:44).

The vow to praise. We meet the vow to praise only rarely in CL psalms, since it belongs properly to the individual lament, as its conclusion. This can be noted in the Babylonian psalms, in which a vow to praise never occurs in the plural, while at the end of individual laments a vow almost always occurs. If, nevertheless, a vow to praise does occur in a number of CL psalms (44:8; 79:13; 80:18; 106:47b; 74:21b; Hos. 6:2; Pss. Sol. 8:33b), that must have special significance. Since the vow in 80:18 echoes the promise of the people at the Shechem assembly (Josh. 24:18, 21, 24), this joining together in a vow to praise can point to the existence of a community's vow to praise, which had its own fixed liturgical place and which has been incorporated here into some of the community laments.

Remarks about specific CL psalms

Psalm 44. This psalm is marked by the bitter contrast between God's past and present activity. The beginning (vv. 1-8) is filled with the praise of God, who helped so wonderfully and powerfully in days of old. But in close juxtaposition stands the complaint that God has abandoned the people in an inconceivably terrible present (vv. 9-22). From the midst of this complaint arises the assertion of these suppliants that despite everything they will hold fast to God (vv. 17-18). The psalm ends in a desperate cry for help (vv. 23-26).

Psalm 60. Many things in this psalm are no longer clear. At its center stands an oracle of salvation (vv. 6-8), which follows after a complaint made in a difficult military crisis (vv. 1-4) and the petition (v. 5). The psalm closes with a confession of confidence, "With God we shall do valiantly . . ." (v. 12).

Psalm 74. This psalm laments the destruction of the sanctuary (vv. 3-9), which is described in detail. Instead of the review of God's deeds of salvation in history, the psalm brings an appeal to the Creator and Lord of history (vv. 12-17). This is an example of how in the Old Testament faith in the Creator arose from anxiety and gave stability to those who were anxious. Here creation is still presented in mythical images (13-14), which still lived on in Israel even after the concept of creation had long since been demythologized.

Psalm 79. The destruction of Jerusalem still clearly rises before our mind's eye from the lament of this psalm: city and temple have been destroyed by the enemy (v. 1) and many people have been killed (vv. 2-3). To destruction has been added shame (v. 4). Deeply shaken, the survivors rise to face the source of the woe: God's burning anger. They plead with God to turn the enemy aside (v. 6) and not to let the children pay for the sins of their fathers. The petitions against the enemy stand out in sharp relief (vv. 6, 10, 12). In a manner very difficult for us to understand, this psalm, with its sharp accusation of God, ends with a vow: "We will give thanks to thee for ever; from generation to generation we will recount thy praise" (v. 13).

Psalm 83. This psalm is very different from Psalm 79. From beginning to end it has its eye on enemies, containing almost nothing but complaints about them and petitions against them! The heaping up of the names of peoples in vv. 6-8 is striking. It can hardly have to do with a specific historical situation. It is possible that all these names of enemies are only bywords for the evildoers who threaten the righteous, and that the psalm really belongs to the IL genre, where the contrast between evildoers and the righteous has its place. It is very likely that Israel recast the ancient CL psalms in this way at a time when it was only a province within an empire and no longer waged war itself.

Psalm 89. The actual complaint begins first with the "but" of v. 38 and continues to the end of the psalm (v. 51). Preceding it is a very elaborate section which corresponds to the review of God's past deeds of salvation. It looks back at one particular deed of God, the covenant with David (vv. 3-4). The psalm is constructed as a poem, the destruction of the royal house (probably 586 B.C.) over against the covenant that God once made with David. This covenant promise is presented in detail (vv. 3-4, 19-37). Inserted into that presentation is a long section of general praise (vv. 5-18) which is a unit in itself and was certainly once an independent psalm of praise.

Psalm 106. This psalm has preserved only vestiges of the community lament. It is a great penitential psalm, which encompasses the entire history of the people. It concludes with a petition to God for the redemption of Israel and the gathering of those who have been scattered among the nations.

2

The Community Psalm of
Narrative Praise (CP)

Despite many individual differences, one common characteristic of all community laments is their cry for deliverance from trouble. But when God broke his silence and came to the aid of the people, when he reversed their trouble and brought deliverance, then his deed had to awaken the jubilation of those who had been liberated, the praise of those who had been saved. This is expressed in the late historical psalm, Psalm 106:

Yet he saved them for his name's sake. . . .
Then they believed his words; they sang his praise (106:8, 12).

This type of praise, which narrates God's deeds, had great significance throughout Israel's entire history, but has barely been transmitted to us in the Psalter. The most compelling reason for this is that the present collection is postexilic. In the postexilic era the people of Israel as a nation no longer experienced such acts of deliverance as are referred to in Ps. 106:12. Therefore at this point we must introduce into our presentation texts from other biblical books.

1. In the early period songs of praise by the people were very brief, only something like a jubilant shout. The oldest song of this sort (one which was never forgotten, however), is the Song of Miriam in Exodus 15:1(-21):

Sing to the Lord, for he has triumphed gloriously;
　the horse and his rider he has thrown into the sea.

This song which celebrates the rescue at the Reed Sea, is a psalm of narrative praise in its simplest form. It consists only of a summons to praise and an account of God's deed, which is expressed in two sentences. This simple form was then expanded in various ways.

2. An expanded form of the community psalm of praise confronts us in Psalms 124 and 129. Though almost unknown, Psalm 124 is able to transport us into the hour in which Israel looked back upon a rescue from very grave trouble and summed up this experience of deliverance in language of relieved praise, understandable to people of all ages:

If it had not been the Lord who was on our side,
　let Israel now say—
if it had not been the Lord who was on our side,
　when men rose up against us,
then they would have swallowed us up alive. . . .
Blessed be the Lord,
　who has not given us as prey to their teeth!
We have escaped as a bird
　from the snare of the fowlers;
the snare is broken,
　and we have escaped! (vv. 1-3, 6-7)

When in their psalms of lament the people looked back to God's earlier deeds of salvation, they thought of the hour in which a song of the redeemed had stirred up "a new song" and had deeply impressed itself on their history. Echoes of this are found in other psalms: 66:8-12; 81:6-7; 85:1-3; 93:3-4; 126:2-3 (cf. Deut. 32:43; Isa. 25:1-5; 26:13-19; Luke 1:68-75).

3. A further development of the brief song of narrative praise is the song of victory. This celebrates Yahweh's victories, praising God as the one who gave victory to Israel. The song of victory also traveled its own path of tradition and had once been in a separate collection. The book mentioned in Numbers 21:14 as "The Book of the Wars of the Lord" must have contained, in part or in its entirety, songs of victory. No song of victory was taken up into the Psalter. This is undoubtedly because after the destruction of Jerusalem in 586 and the Babylonian exile Israel no longer experienced any victories for centuries.

How the song of victory could develop from a brief composition about as long as the Song of Miriam into a great, extensive artistic work is shown when one compares the song of victory which the Philistines sang (Judg. 16:23-24) with the magnificent Song of Deborah (Judges 5). The songs of victory —no matter how strange this seems to us—were also originally worship songs. They had their fixed place in the conduct of the war of Yahweh, the holy war which began with consulting Yahweh for an oracle and ended with a song that praised Yahweh's deed. In Israel's early period there surely once existed many songs of victory. Besides the great Song of Deborah, however, only fragments and reminiscences have been preserved (Josh. 10:12-13; Ps. 126:3; 118:15-16; motifs in Psalms 18; 68; 149. Judith 16 is a late imitation). Reminiscent of the songs of victory are many Easter hymns of the Christian church, such as "Christ Is Arisen."

4. Part of the song of victory is the description of God's epiphany (Judg. 5:4-5; Ps. 18:7-15; 68:7-8; Judith 16:15), i.e. the description of God's appearance which shakes heaven and earth, when he comes to help his people. This description also frequently appears outside songs of victory (Hab. 3:3-15; Pss. 77:16-19; 97:2-5; 114; Deuteronomy 33; Isa. 30:27-33; 59:15b-

20; 63:1-6; Mic. 1:3-4; Nah. 1:3b-6). In the description we always find the same features. God's epiphany is very often connected with the event of the Reed Sea. By means of this connection a very ancient motif, which with its mythically-colored language reminds one of the Egyptian and Babylonian psalms accompanying the epiphany of a deity, is now employed to celebrate the entirely new and unique experience of Israel: Yahweh's heaven-and-earth-shaking advent for the purpose of liberating his people from their enemies.

A review of the community psalms of lament and praise

Among the psalms discussed or mentioned to this point, there is not a single one which has been prominent in the Christian tradition, not one which is reckoned among the best-known and beloved psalms in our congregations today. There is good reason for this. These psalms are all the direct or indirect echo of what happened to Israel as a people among peoples in the days of its political heights and depths. They speak extensively of victories and defeats, of pressure from enemies and liberation from enemies. This could not be transferred to the history of Christ's church in a direct manner. Neither can these psalms immediately and directly become the Christian community's petition and lament, its praise and jubilation. Only a forced interpretation which would remove itself from the simple and clear meaning of these texts could expound these psalms in the form they now have as prayers of a Christian community.

Yet whoever has followed our explanation and presentation of these community psalms and has read the psalms themselves will have recognized that in them we come upon the foundation which enables us to understand the entire breadth and depth of the Psalms. For what the people of Israel experienced *in their own history* as the deeds of God, evoking their jubilant praise or their pleading lament, formed the very foundation of their calling on God in praise and lament. We will not really understand the psalms which are dear and precious to the Christian community if we seek to understand them and pray with them apart from this basis, apart from the people of Israel's lament and praise as they grew from their own history.

Therefore we do not wish to offer a Christian interpretation of the psalms we have so far heard. We should first simply listen to them and let ourselves be affected by the mighty rhythm of these prayers of Israel as they come out of the depths and heights of its national history. They will then speak their message to us together with the other more familiar psalms. They will be present when we hear the 23rd Psalm or the 46th; we will no longer lose sight of this foundation. Later, then, some things will be said about how they relate to and belong to the totality of the Psalter for us. For the Psalter is a unity.

3

The Individual Psalm of Lament (IL)

The texts

The individual psalm of lament is by far the most frequent type found in the Psalter. About 50 belong to this genre: Psalms 3-17 (with the exception of 8; 9; 15); 22-28 (except 24); 31; 35-43 (except 37; 40A); 51-64 (except 60); 69; 71; 73; (77); 86; 88; (94); 102; 109; (120); 130. Outside the Psalter: Lamentations 3; Jeremiah 11; 15; 17; 18; 20. Elements of the IL genre are the basis for many parts of the Book of Job. Individual elements also occur in many other passages.

The liturgical action

The individual psalm of lament is also a prayer used in worship. But because the forms and variant forms of IL psalms are so abundant, the liturgical action of which they are a part must not be defined too narrowly. The story of Samuel's mother at the beginning of 1 Samuel shows us most clearly what place this sort of psalm had in ancient Israel. A person in great trouble came to the sanctuary and poured out her heart to God. In answer to her prayer she received—in this case from a priest—the assurance that God had heard her. And this assurance effected a change in the person who had lamented: she was convinced that God had hearkened to her. Isaiah 38, with its story of the sickness of King Hezekiah, is another example. In this case the king prayed to God from his sickbed for healing, and the prophet Isaiah was sent to him, to announce that God had heard him. This example shows that the individual psalm of lament, even though it is a liturgical prayer, can be prayed not *only* in the temple—something we learn also from many other passages. Of course the liturgical action to which both the prayer of lament and the oracle of salvation (God's response), belong, is presupposed in the psalms of lament in the book of Psalms. And there are psalms (e.g. 6 and 28) in which one can sense very directly an action which made the supplicants certain that they had been heard. The Psalms themselves, however, present only the one side of what was happening—the prayer of the one who lamented. The answer given by a man of God (priest or a sanctuary prophet) is not reproduced in the psalms themselves. Most of them, however, indicate a turning point or break in the complaint—which is understandable only when one realizes that the suppliants received a word of comfort from outside themselves. It is possible that in addition we are to assume that there were services for special situations: in the case of a person unjustly accused, or ill, or seeking asylum at a sanctuary. But at present this is more supposition than a solid foundation for understanding these psalms.

An example: Psalm 13

This is a very brief, simple psalm, which however just for that reason can beautifully exhibit the basic characteristic of this genre. As we hear this psalm we must presuppose that over the course of centuries it received the form in which it has been transmitted to us. One may assume that long before it was written and added to a collection of psalms it summed up and carried along the sorrow and anxiety of many generations. Further, one may take for granted that the very words themselves were in various ways actually lived and suffered, and were suffused by the sounds of the suffering people who used them to bring their pain to God. In this long and moving prehistory the psalm received its extremely succinct form, one in which each word represents many sentences, many chains of thought.

The psalm begins with the fourfold question of "How long?" It is the "How long?" of the complaint directed to God which we also found in the community psalm of lament. It is the very human, very natural "How long?" which sufferers speak when they can no longer endure continuing pain, pressure, and the absence of prospects for improvement. We meet it often also in Babylonian psalms of lament; it is neither specifically biblical nor specifically Israelite; it is entirely human. For that reason, because it is so very human, this complaint of "How long?" became a specifically liturgical expression down through the ages, from primitive religions through the time of Babylon and Israel until the Christian hymn's "Ah, how long in anguish shall my spirit languish?" *("Jesu, meine Freude").*

The four questions are clearly divided into questions about God, self, and the enemy. The first two have God as subject:

How long, O Lord? Wilt thou forget me forever?
  How long wilt thou hide thy face from me? (v. 1)

This is the accusation against God. The question directs its full force first of all (and it is not accidental that this first part of the complaint is doubled) toward that place where the difficulties of the troubled must have had their origin. The questions speak about God in a very human manner: "How long wilt thou forget me . . . ? How long wilt thou hide thy face from me?" But it is precisely these human questions which indicate the genuineness of a relationship to God—a relationship in which joy, happiness, freedom, and health can only be understood as dependent upon God's attention to and participation in human life. But if these qualities are absent, then God is absent.

The complaint-about-self, the I-complaint comes from having first looked toward God. "How long must I bear pain?" the suppliant asks, at the same time directing the complaint to God. Who else could measure what the sufferer has to bear? The third aspect of the complaint does the same thing: "How long shall my enemy be exalted over me?" (v. 2) How much longer? After all, the triumph of enemies over those who are righteous is an accusation against God. How long will this go on? We never learn what was disturbing the suppliant. The threefold complaint does not even give a clue. We never even learn this information in individual psalms of lament which are much more detailed than Psalm 13. Only in a very few are the symptoms of the sufferings described more clearly.

At this point we meet a characteristic feature of this group of psalms. Trouble is what the suppliant brings to God in the lament, but this was not what *we* understand as trouble. It is not *symptoms* of the psalmist's troubles which are mentioned. Therefore trouble is here not what is perceived by the senses on the surface of one's feelings. Rather it is more the disturbance of healthiness or wholeness, something which shows itself not primarily in symptoms but in the interrelationships which characterize being alive: in the relations of the lamenter to God, to self, and to others.

These three relationships are what are unfolded in the psalms of lament, not certain symptoms which have been separated and isolated from them. This is why we learn so little about the trouble of the sufferers—what is commonly understood as suffering. And this is also why these psalms penetrated the life of the community so deeply and broadly. They created a tradition and a history of this genre (psalms of lament) which can scarcely be equalled by any others. The lament directed to God by the individual is not only the most frequent type of psalm in the Psalter, it has a significance for the entire Old Testament, as can be seen especially in the laments of Jeremiah (Jer. 11; 15; 17; 18; 20) and in the Book of Job.

The complaint is followed by the petition. Here again we find the bipartite form of petition already observed in the CL psalms. First the petitioner prays to God in v. 3 for him to turn and help: "Consider and answer me . . . !" (This corresponds precisely to the first two statements of the complaint.) Then the psalmist asks, "lighten my eyes," an indirect petition for God's intervention—for only when God gave help would the psalmist's eyes again shine. When people in trouble ask God to "consider," this does not mean they are denying God's divinity in the sense of excluding something from God's omniscience. Rather, this petition shows that human beings cannot always stand uniformly near to God. They experience that God is remote, and their calls to God mean that they want to come near to God again. Also in this case the petition is bolstered by reasons which intend to make it more persuasive. Whereas the petition as a whole corresponds to the accusation against God, the two motifs of the petition correspond to the second (I-complaint) and third (complaint about the enemy) parts of the complaint. In the clause ". . . lest I sleep the sleep of death," pain and sorrow (v. 2) are understood as steps toward death. Death is not only the end of physical life; it is a power which projects itself into life. The other motif (reference to the enemy's triumph) has already been explained in the section dealing with the complaint.

However, the "but" which now follows in v. 5 indicates a reversal, a turning point. The lamenter has taken a step beyond the complaint. By a declaration of confidence the psalmist has entered territory where the complaint can be silenced. Powers which threaten to destroy the suppliant's life are not the only powers that exist. There is one power in which the psalmist can trust: "But I have trusted in thy steadfast love." Attached to this declaration of trust reversing the complaint is a promise which at the same time also forms the conclusion of the psalm. Its first sentence is formulated as a wish, but it is more than a wish. In the newly-won confidence based on God's goodness, the petitioner—with daring faith—now has stepped forth into the hour of deliverance, in which he will rejoice in God's help. What was expressed as a wish becomes in the second sentence a declaration: "I will sing to the Lord because he has dealt bountifully with me."

In these last statements of Psalm 13 the secret of the individual psalm of lament is revealed, if only partially. What becomes apparent is the fact that a reversal occurred while the lament was being prayed. This reversal appears throughout the entire genre. To be sure, it appears in various degrees and in very different ways. Yet the fact itself cannot be overlooked, and is commonly acknowledged and kept in mind when the Psalms are interpreted.

The explanation for this reversal inside a psalm of lament is to be found if we look in the direction of the oracle of salvation. In fact, we spoke of this at this same point in connection with community laments. The secret behind the reversal is, however, thereby explained only one step further. It will never be possible to clarify completely how, over a long period of time, and in such a variety of different psalms, prayers could be prayed in such a way that within them this reversal took place. The lamenters, in the brief space of a prayer, stepped out of complaint into trust, into the certainty that their prayers had been heard, into an anticipation of the jubilation experienced by those who have been delivered. More is at work here than a certain cultic background to the prayers. More is at work than a "change in mood" (many commentaries "explain" it as such). In this well-attested reversal from complaint to trust or to praise of God, we are dealing with the direct witness—the direct reflection—of an intervention from outside, from beyond; we are dealing with an activity of God which actually had been experienced and which was concretized, as a result of such experience, in the structure of these psalms.

In surveying the entire genre of psalms we will find that at this point a clear barrier is set up against our blithely assuming that all we have to do is simply join in the praying. It is all the more important for us to see from the outset this single most important characteristic feature of this group of psalms, a feature which makes it without question a witness to God's activity.

The structure

In their main parts, IL psalms conform to the pattern of CL psalms. Both consist of complaint and petition from trouble; both are directed to God. Hence the IL genre has these components: *address* (often with an introductory call for help), *complaint* in its threefold form, *petition* with motifs and words which express the fact that a reversal of the complaint has occurred.

But an IL psalm also has special, very clearly discernible characteristics of its own. These are based on the fact that troubles of individuals are of a different nature than those of an entire community or people. Accordingly the reversal of an individual's troubles is different and is expected in a different way. The gap between trouble and rescue—between suffering and the reversal of suffering—ordinarily shows up smaller on the horizon of an individual's life than on the horizon of the life of a people. That is the basis for the most important difference in structure between the two: the IL psalm permits us to recognize (to a great extent within the psalm itself) the reversal from complaint to trust, or to the confidence of having been heard. It is entirely understandable and reasonable that in this temporally broader horizon of the CL psalms the suppliants' view toward God and God's actions should include the past. Therefore a review of past help became a regular feature in the CL psalms (cf. Psalm 80), where in the IL psalms it occurs only rarely (e.g. Psalm 22; 143). In its place the entire emphasis in the IL's looking to God is on the confession of trust, with the frequent addition of words expressing certainty of having been heard. In their concluding parts a great number of IL psalms turn into words of praise to God. In the CL psalms that almost never happens. The vow to praise is a regular feature of the IL genre—whenever it is missing, a reason for its omission can usually be found.

There are great differences between different IL psalms. We may speak of petitions which have been heard whenever psalms' conclusions are marked by the certainty of having been heard or by the praise of God. We may speak of petitions which are still open in the case of psalms which are still waiting for a response from God. Various types of IL psalms can be distinguished according to whether one of their parts is especially emphasized or whether it determines the entire psalm. The parts which can move far to the forefront in the IL genre are above all the complaint about enemies and the confession of confidence.

Types of individual laments

a) Only in a few of the IL psalms does the personal suffering of the lamenter stand so clearly in the forefront that we can recognize the trouble. Often individual statements of the complaint permit us to recognize sickness as the *cause of suffering*, but in hardly any psalm can it be definitely stated that sickness is the *only* reason for the lament. Hence an identifiable group of sickness psalms cannot be isolated. Psalms 22; 38; 102 speak a great deal about sickness; in others only single statements permit us to infer sickness. In the case of these, however, it cannot be said whether or not they are meant in a metaphorical sense. The petition "Heal me, O Lord" cannot always be assumed to be the petition of an ill person. Likewise the petitions "Vindicate me" or "Plead my cause" (my legal case) do not always presuppose that a person has been accused or sentenced.

Attempts have been made to interpret a group of IL psalms (esp. Psalms 7; 35; 37; 69) as prayers of an innocent person unjustly accused. That is possible, but still uncertain, because in the Psalms suffering and injustice are remarkably close to one another. A suffering person may call out to God from the same situation, "Heal me!", "Free me!", or "Vindicate me!" Hence all the attempts to attach individual psalms to individual situations have not been completely successful. As we try to understand these psalms we must be satisfied with the knowledge that we are not here observing at firsthand the sufferings of those who brought these complaints before God. Rather, that suffering has passed through a prism and has been broken up, as it were, into the traditional parts of these psalms. These traditional parts enabled individual sufferers to put their own personal suffering into a lament which had been used already by their parents and grandparents. And these forms let them hide the suffering which was theirs and theirs alone in a lament which had been brought before God a thousand times before.

b) The preceding comments hold true particularly for the great complex of complaints *about enemies,* which form by far the strongest and most frequent motif in this most numerous of psalm genres. In Psalm 13 enemies stand only on the edge of things, so to speak, yet they are an essential feature in the prayer. Also in Psalm 23, a psalm of trust, enemies are not missing. While the CL psalms dealt obviously with political opponents (enemy nations), in the IL psalms it is unclear who these enemies are—despite the fact that so many statements in these psalms deal with them.

Since what is said of enemies is so similar and always expresses only what is typical (never what is particular), by and large all these psalms are thinking of the same enemies. These prayers speak of *one* activity of these enemies, the one which is important to them and of which they speak so often (in about 36 psalms) with many words and metaphors: Enemies threaten the petitioners; they have conspired against them; they seek their ruin. Three metaphors are repeated again and again: they set a net or trap for the petitioners (e.g. 140:4-5); they threaten them like wild beasts (e.g. 17:11-12); they attack them like warriors (7:13). In addition, they make league against the righteous and forge plans against them (56:6); they surround them with threatening purposes (22:12-13, 16); they hate them (25:19). The enemies' words keep pace with their deeds. They preface the deeds they threaten to do with scorn and mockery (42:10; 69:9; 89:51). They evidence blatant, unrestrained joy at the sufferers' misfortune (35:15; 13:4). They feed on the misfortune of the righteous (22:17b; 35:21).

In addition to this sort of activity and talk against the suppliants, in many psalms there are general statements which declare the enemies to be evildoers, false to God and people. Hence they are also called transgressors, hypocrites, wicked persons, fools, and the like. In Luther's translation we often find the word *godless* used to describe them. This word, however, cannot be taken in its modern sense. A theoretical, fundamental atheism was not yet possible in the world of the Psalms. Nevertheless the appellation "god-less" (which has no exact correspondence in the Hebrew text) points to a feature of these wicked people which is often emphasized: "The fool says in his heart, 'There is no God'" (Ps. 14:1). This statement is not meant as a theoretical denial of God's existence, but is a judgment of the righteous concerning their opponents who do not take God seriously in their hearts; ". . . they have rebelled against thee" (5:10); "for the wicked boasts of the desires of his heart . . . and renounces the Lord" (10:3; also 28:5; 36:1; 52:7; 54:3; 55:19; 73:11 and elsewhere also). In addition their general corruption and wickedness is often mentioned (14:1, 3-4; 26:10; 28:4; 36:4; 52:1-4; 55:10-11 and elsewhere).

These are all *very general* designations of the petitioners' enemies. They do not permit us to recognize who is meant thereby. Previous attempts to determine this more precisely have not been successful (e.g. Mowinckel wished to interpret them, in keeping with Babylonian parallels, as soothsayers). But this much can be said with certainty: the enmity of these enemies, even though they usually form a group, is directed always and only at the one who speaks in the psalm. This person is the *only* one who is attacked. We are never told, not even by slight intimation, that this person belongs to a group and that the attack is aimed at a group. This is connected with the other feature (equally surprising), that this individual who is threatened by enemies is delivered up to them in seeming impotence. The idea of putting up a defense does not occur—not in the slightest. The many metaphors of conflict which we meet in the complaints about enemies are completely one-sided; they are always focused only on the opponent. The *only* fighter is the opponent, never the one who does the lamenting. It is clear that both the individual who laments and the enemies belong to the same community. They visit one another (41:5-6); the enemies speak with the lamenter in a friendly manner (55:21). Often it is this which constitutes the complaint: a neighbor or a friend is the one who has turned against the suppliant.

The psalmist cannot trust their friendly words, for they are lies and falsehoods (55:21). The enemies have smooth tongues but enmity lurks in the background.

In all these statements about enemies one thing seems clear: here is a community which is breaking apart. It is marked by conflict in which a very powerful group confronts one which is helpless. This helpless group has no sort of organization, but includes only people who stand alone, who are indeed continually being pressured by the others. However, it is obvious that the enmity has not reached the point where the impotent ones are actually being physically attacked or destroyed. In all this the real reason for the conflict is their respective relations to God. In the opinion of the suppliants (those who call themselves "the pious" or "the righteous") the others do not take God seriously. But this is at the same time the deepest vexation *(Anfechtung)* of the suppliants: the others are able to continue to exist in their "godlessness" unpunished. They are able to mock the righteous with impunity (esp. Psalm 73).

All these features are understandable in the postexilic age in which Israel was merely a province of an empire, when membership in the people of Israel was consequently no longer identical with membership in the community faithful to Israel's God. One may surmise that those who are meant by the term "evildoers" are the group in the population which adapted itself in its entire life-style to its pagan environment. (We know about one feature of such acculturation: after the land came under Greek hegemony, elements of Greek culture entered the people's life, as is especially evident in the giving of Greek names.) The enemies were the people who no longer held strictly to the Torah; instead, they thought enlightened thoughts—and also apparently to a large extent belonged to a rich, ruling upper class.

This explanation of the opposition between the righteous who lament in these psalms and their enemies is, to be sure, not conclusively established; it can only be surmised. But it is the best way to clarify the consistent characteristics in the descriptions of "evildoers," namely *everything* which is said in the complaints about the enemies is understandable in this sort of situation. The same conflict between the righteous and evildoers is found also to a great extent in the Book of Proverbs. In this case also it is in the later, younger layer of proverbs in which we hear, in endless variation, the struggle between the righteous and evildoers (or "fools," as they are most often called, as in Ps. 14:1). This contrast would seem to belong to the same age and the same situation in society.

From this perspective the description of the enemies of those who lament in the IL psalms is understandable; also understandable is the petition for the destruction of enemies—a petition which is so difficult for us to repeat as members of the church of Christ, and which in so many of these psalms is directed to God. Those who held fast to the God of their fathers, who saw in God's commandments the directives for their lives, and who lived out of joy in God's word—all those were in the minority in their own land. They were "the poor." Others had the power. They took a position on the side of God and God's cause, and were convinced that this cause would stand or fall with them, the righteous. In their Old Testament situation the possibility did not yet exist for God to speak his yes beyond death to the one who held fast to him. The case for or against the righteous *had to be* decided on this earth, in the lifetimes of individual righteous persons. No other possibility as yet existed for them. For this reason there was also no possibility to glorify and magnify God in suffering and in death.

This is where the boundary line for faith in God in the Old Testament stood. The Old Testament's God was a God of the living; at death the relationship to God ceased completely.

This is often mentioned in the Psalms as a reason held up to move God to hearken to a petition. "The dead do not praise the Lord" (Ps. 115:17); all praise of God ceases at death. That is the real reason why the case between the pious person and the evildoer must be decided on earth while both are still living. If a righteous person dies in misery and a godless person triumphs—if it is possible for this godless person to continue to live happily despite rebellion against God while the righteous person ends in misery and ruin—then that could not have been understood in those days in *any other way* than as a decision of God against the righteous and for the evildoer, and with that the foundation of Old Testament faith in God would have been really shattered. Hence part of the afflicted person's supplication for rescue from misery (and a necessary concomitant) was the petition against the enemies. If God heard this petition, then God's hearkening had two sides: if God intervened for the righteous, this was at the same time an intervention against the enemies.

With the coming of Christ a fundamental change took place for the Christian community precisely at this point. Suffering and dying, which until then could be understood only in negative terms (as God's turning away from a person), through Christ received the possibility of having positive significance. God spoke a yes to suffering and dying; Christ could by his suffering and dying glorify and praise God. The same thing can happen also when people follow Jesus. With this the corresponding relationship which righteous persons have to their enemies has been broken. For to those who cry to God from any trouble in which the enemies of God have a hand the possibility is now given of experiencing God's yes, God's affirmation (also in suffering—even in dying), without having to see God intervene against their enemies. Petitions for enemies' destruction (in fact every petition against enemies in general) have once and for all been taken away from Christ's congregation. As a sign of this, Christ cried out to God on the cross not *against* his enemies, but *for* them: "'Father, forgive them; for they know not what they do'" (Luke 23:34).

Of course there are also great differences among the Psalms themselves. For example, the great Psalm 22 contains, to be sure, an extensive description of enemies, but not one single petition against them. On the other hand, Psalm 109 consists of almost nothing but petitions against enemies. Between these extremes are many intermediary forms of petitions and complaints about enemies. In light of all we have said, it is proper that distinctions be made in reading and praying the Psalms within the church. In other words, psalms that have their full center of gravity in petitions directed against enemies recede into the background in the reading and praying of the Christian church.

c) The *Confession of sins* is prominent in only a very small group of IL psalms. This has its place as part of the reason why the petition ought to be heard. The actual petition is always for deliverance from trouble; often a petition for forgiveness is added, but only rarely does it become central in a psalm (as in Psalm 51). In the Christian church these so-called penitential psalms (6; 32; 38; 51; 69; 102; 130) were often given special emphasis. However, the confession of sins and the petition for forgiveness of sins are rare in IL psalms. This fact is deeply-rooted in the Psalms' understanding of human beings. External well-being and inner relationship to God are here very closely connected one to the other. If a person sins against God, this is evidenced by that person's outward condition; likewise, a blow one receives points to a transgression. Thus especially sickness and sin are seen as closely related. This view extends even into the New Testament. Hence what lamenting persons ask for, the hearkening and helping intervention of God, is at the same time forgiveness. It encompasses forgiveness within itself. Therefore when in Psalm 13 the lamenting person says, "Consider . . . , " the psalmist is asking for God to turn toward him, and that is in itself a demonstration of mercy and pardon. A special petition for the forgiveness of sins is not necessary in this case because it is included in the petition for God's consideration. But it cannot then be said—as is often done—that the psalms in which the petition of forgiveness of sins is expressly mentioned stand for that reason closer to the New Testament than for example Psalms 13 or 22, in which this petition is not expressed. What is basically meant by forgiveness of sins, namely God's gracious consideration of and turning toward a person who has erred, can also be present without being specially formulated in words. It may be assumed that such psalms in which we hear about forgiveness of sins often and with emphasis, such as Psalm 51, are late psalms, from a time in which the unity of psychosomatic existence before God was no longer taken for granted, as it had been earlier.

Beside these psalms in which suppliants confess their sins and beg for forgiveness stand psalms which *maintain the petitioner's innocence,* such as 5; 7; 17; 26 and others. These psalms are designed to move God precisely because the suppliants assert innocence of an evil deed. If in this connection we hear in Psalm 26, "I wash my hands in innocence, and go about thy altar, O Lord" (v. 6), reference is thereby made to a worship practice in which an assertion of innocence in a specific situation took ritual form. It is important for our understanding of these psalms to realize that here sin and being free from sin are not yet so generalized as in New Testament usage. In a single psalm genre, and in connection with the reasons why God should hearken to the petition, we can find sometimes a confession of sins, sometimes an assertion of innocence. There are times when persons who step out of trouble into the presence of God confess their sin; there are times when they assert their innocence. They are not always sinners and saints at one and the same time.

d) The element which is so important for the IL, the *confession of confidence* (cf. what was said above about Ps. 13:6) became an independent type of psalm, the psalm of trust, in the following cases: Pss. 23; 27:1-6; 62; 63; 71; 131. These psalms, especially Psalm 23, have rightly received special significance in the Christian church. Unfortunately they have, in the process, often been misinterpreted and watered down. Trust in God, which received a unique formulation in these psalms, is not a human attitude. The metaphors in which it is presented in Psalm 23 are not idyllic. Rather, these psalms can be rightly understood only against the background of the psalms of lament, from which they are derived. They are all spoken in the presence of dire threat ("Even though I walk through the valley of the shadow of death . . ."), and they, as a whole, represent a movement to meet this threat. In all of this what is happening is what an interpreter described in the following way: "One throws oneself into God's arms."

Community psalms of trust also occur, especially Psalm 123; in addition also 125; 126; and, with variation, Psalm 90.

Psalm 123, one of the great artistic masterpieces of the Psalms, is a brief, but mighty prayer, consisting really of *one* elaborated metaphor:

Behold, as the eyes of servants look to the hand of their master,
as the eyes of a maid to the hand of her mistress,
so our eyes look to the Lord our God,
    till he have mercy upon us (v. 2).

This psalm begins as the suppliant turns to God, and, after the image is elaborated, there follows only one petition. "Have mercy upon us, O Lord" (v. 3), with a motif which only hints at the complaint. This psalm, like few others, can make clear what the Old Testament means by prayer. It is nothing but the suffering creature's stretching forth toward the Creator. In this turning to God both things which the metaphor expresses are present: (1) turning to the Lord, who, even when punishing or smiting still remains the Lord, respected in majesty, and at the same time (2) turning to the condescending grace of the Savior from whom alone the sufferer can receive salvation and healing. If a person reads this psalm repeatedly and prays it with an understanding of what is happening in it, then that person will become amazed at this complete unification of liturgical praying and direct, reality-drenched living. This is how it is with the Psalms.

4

The Individual Psalm of
Narrative Praise (IP)

The entire Bible is filled with the praise of God. It extends from the indirect, hidden praise of the Creator in its first pages to the songs of the saints at the edge of time in the accounts of John's Revelation. The gospel of Luke begins with psalms of praise, and Christianity's first hymns were songs which celebrated the resurrection victory. God's praise can be expressed in a number of ways, and psalms of praise are central to this expression. It is an illusion to imagine that lament outweighs praise in the Psalms simply because statistically there are so many psalms of lament, for in a great number of IL psalms the lamenting changes to praise. Also in CL psalms praise has a place of its own in the review of God's past saving acts. Above all, however, the confession of praise by those who have been delivered stands at the beginning of biblical historiography and continues from that point throughout the entire history.

The narrative or confessing psalm of praise by the individual corresponds to the psalm of lament by the individual. They belong together like two acts of a drama. At the end of an IL psalm we hear the vow to praise, "I will sing to the Lord, because he has dealt bountifully with me" (e.g. Ps. 13:6). That vow to praise is now fulfilled in the psalm of narrative praise. What was promised and vowed there is carried out and fulfilled here.

The texts

Psalms of narrative praise by the individual are found in Pss. 9; 18; 30; 31:7-8, 19-24; 32; 40:1-12; 66:13-20; 92; (107); 116; (118); 138; also Jonah 2; Lam. 3:25-58; Job 33:26-28; Sir. 51; Pss. Sol. 15:1-6; 16:1-15; Song of the Three Young Men 1:65-66; Odes Sol. 25; 29; the collection of Hymns from the Dead Sea Scrolls *(Hôdāyôt)* contains further developments of this genre.

The liturgical action

The liturgical activity which accompanied this group of psalms can be very clearly discerned in the psalms themselves. The Hebrew designation of the genre is *tôdāh,* a word meaning both "praise" and at the same time "sacrifice of praise." Hence we can conclude that originally this type of psalm was a statement which accompanied a sacrifice of praise. Psalm 66:13-14 expresses the connection:

I will come into thy house with burnt offerings;
  I will pay thee my vows,
that which my lips uttered
  and my mouth promised when I was in trouble.

The following verse (15) refers to the sacrifice which the worshiper offered; then he says:

Come and hear, all you who fear God,
  and I will tell what he has done for me.

What follows now is narrative praise, i.e. an account of the wonderful deliverance from trouble which the worshiper had experienced. Psalm 22:26 refers to a sacrificial meal eaten on such an occasion. According to Ps. 116:19 such sacrificial celebrations were observed in the courtyard of the temple. The oral narration of the deliverance, which together with the sacrifice was part of the fulfillment of a vow, presupposes the presence of a circle of listeners who are often mentioned in the Psalms. They are sometimes summoned to join in with the praise of the one telling what God has done:

O magnify the Lord with me,
    and let us exalt his name together! (Ps. 34:3)

In the liturgy Psalm 118, vv. 22-25 are perhaps the response of the circle of listeners. The narrative about trouble and deliverance which was spoken (or sung) before a group thereby received the character of a confession or declaration (*hôdāh* can also mean "confession" or "declaration"), just as the community's narrative praise became the recital of a historical creed.

Gradually, however, the connection of this psalm of narrative or confessing praise with a sacrifice of praise was loosened; it detached itself and became independent. This is shown by Psalms 34 and 92, which have combined with motifs of wisdom speech and therefore can hardly have been accompanied by a sacrifice of praise. The fact that at the same time the IP genre retained its significance for worship is indicated in Psalms 107 and 118, two liturgies in which an IP form provides the central section—each time in a different way.

The structure

If visible anywhere, then it is in this psalm genre that the solid structure of a genre can be seen by anyone who (even without any previous knowledge) simply lines up the texts listed above alongside one another. The IP psalm is related to the IL psalm by means of the vow to praise which the latter brings at its conclusion. In fact, the conclusion of many IL psalms is identical with the introduction of many IP psalms. The vow to praise at the end of the IL becomes the announcement at the beginning of the IP, as a comparison of Pss. 13:6 or 56:13 with 30:1 indicates. The most frequent introduction to the IP psalm is this announcement, as in Ps. 34:1:

I will bless the Lord at all times;
    his praise shall continually be in my mouth.

There follows upon this introduction an introductory summary of the narrative:

. . . because he has heard my voice and my supplications (116:1).

The main part is then the account which confesses God's deed, almost always divided into a review of the crisis and an account of the rescue. Here trouble is often described as being enslaved or being in death, while rescue is correspondingly described as liberation from death. Here also the correspondence to the individual lament is very clear. The three parts of the account of the rescue correspond to the parts of the IL:

IL	IP
call (with complaint)	"To you I cried."
petition for God's turning toward	"You heard me."
petition for God's intervention	"You have drawn me up out of the pit."

After this central section comes the conclusion of the psalm, which can take many variant forms, but which always aims at praising God. As Ps. 40:3 puts it,

He put a new song in my mouth,
  a song of praise to our God.

Here God's rescuing action is tied very closely to the resultant
praise (as also in Ps. 30:11). We observed that the most important feature in the IL psalms is the change to trust, quiet-
ness, certainty, or praise. This is precisely what is reflected in
the IP psalms. They are all dominated not only by the fact
that God reversed suffering in the life of the individual who
spoke them, but also by the surprising, overwhelming miracle
of this reversal:

For his anger is but for a moment,
  and his favor is for a lifetime.
Weeping may tarry for the night,
  but joy comes with the morning (30:5).

Often the vow to praise returns again at the conclusion, but
then mostly in an expanded form, stating that the praise of
God will not cease as soon as this confession has been completed. It will continue; it cannot remain silent (30:12). The
life which had been restored by God's intervention now has
meaning as a life of praise. Cf. Pss. 92:15; 118:17; Isa. 38:18-19.

Sheol cannot thank thee;
  death cannot praise thee. . . .
The living, the living, he thanks thee . . . (Isa. 38:18-19).

At the end narrative praise usually changes into descriptive
praise. Psalm 40:5 shows how the one grows out of the other:

Thou hast multiplied, O Lord my God,
  thy wondrous deeds and thy thoughts toward us;
  none can compare with thee!

The view of the person who has personally experienced God's deliverance searches out the broad expanse of God's activity: Pss. 18:30-31; 116:15; 118:5-8; Jonah 2:9.

Narrative praise, as a response to God's deed by a person who has been liberated, heard, healed, and delivered, is something which has occurred everywhere where people live their lives in the presence of a personal god. Even in the prayers of primitive peoples we find this (see F. Heiler, *Prayer*, trans. and ed. by S. McComb [New York: Oxford University Press, 1958], p. 39). Here we find the most simple form: a *single* narrative statement with the address. A prayer of the Khonds (Africa) is, "You have rescued me, O God!" Some form of narrative praise is found in most religions. Among the Egyptian and Babylonian psalms there are a few very close parallels to the IP psalms, but they are rare. What predominates in both these religions is general descriptive praise of God.

Reminiscences of narrative praise are found also in the New Testament: Luke 1:46-55; 2:29-32; Acts 2:24. Acts 2:11 certainly refers to Ps. 22:22. This shows that in narrative praise we find a root of proclamation. It is also possible to find a reflection of the structure of the IP psalm also in the structure of the epistle to the Romans. But a place where this structure is undeniably present is Luther's hymn, "Dear Christians, One and All Rejoice," as also in other hymns of the church (e.g. "I cried to him in time of need," from the third stanza of "All Praise to God Who Reigns Above"). I will only make mention of an entirely different development: in the *Confessions* of Augustine all the basic features of the psalm of confessing or narrative praise occur with great clarity.

These points can show that the individual psalm of narrative praise (as well as that of the community) has a very special significance and stands peculiarly at the center of the entire psalm material. These psalms are the immediate echoes of

God's acts which have been experienced by the community or by an individual member of God's people.

An example: Psalm 30

Verse 1a. Verse 1 of Psalm 30 brings the announcement, "I will extol thee, O Lord. . . ." Such is the significance of the psalm of confessing praise which then follows: God is to be exalted by it. God is extolled. God becomes great when the deed which he performed in someone's daily life is joyfully confessed in the presence of others by the person who can bear witness to it.

Verses 1b-3. The introductory summary of this particular psalm does not consist of the more usual single sentence. In this case at the beginning the worshiper felt compelled to relate *everything* that happened. Hence in this introduction the entire psalm is anticipated, even though the first sentence would have sufficed (". . . for thou hast drawn me up"). But now the psalmist had to add immediately that this all happened in the very presence of enemies, who could no longer exult over the worshiper's fall (cf. 13:5). Verse 2 tells how this happened by placing right next to each other the two events in which the tide was turned and the reversal took place: the *cry* and the *answer*, the suppliant cry of the person who lamented to God and the answer of God who hearkened to this supplication:

O Lord my God, I cried to thee for help,
    and thou hast healed me (v. 2).

In this verse the entire faith of the Psalms is expressed. This faith grew out of thousands of experiences of an open door through which suppliants spoke to God out of all sorts of human trouble. This supplication did not disappear into thin air.

In verse 3 God's deed is described as rescue from death. Here what was already said in connection with Ps. 13:3 (cf. p. 59) is still more clear: death is a power which reaches into life. A person can, despite the fact that he or she is still physically living and breathing, nevertheless suffer such pain, anxiety, despair, or lethargy that this condition can no longer really be called life. In this the psalmist saw death at work—the person who suffers thus is in the clutches of death. Therefore anyone who is liberated from such is really rescued from death.

Verses 4-5. In these verses we hear a call to the surrounding listeners to join in praising God. What happened in this "rescue from death" was, for the worshiper, more than a fortunate turn of events for one individual. In this event a human life was torn from the power of death, and therefore the event also has significance for the circle of the living. The individual to whom this happened represents only a specific instance of the occurrence of a victory which has much wider significance. Hence one individual's small destiny becomes universally important and meaningful because that individual becomes a witness to a power of life to which others can cling if death should clutch at them. So the one individual person in the joy of liberation includes others in this joy:

Sing praises to the Lord, O you his saints. . . .

A great many psalms of descriptive praise begin with this imperative call to praise (see below). In this psalm of narrative praise we see how a summons to praise God can go forth from an individual who has experienced God's deed and therefore received the authority to draw others into his or her praise. The psalmist knows that deliverance is possible, and can prove it. This is actually done in the beautiful statement which describes the reversal—the reversal from weeping to joy (v. 5).

Verses 6-10. These verses bring a review of the crisis. In Psalm 30 this review is in expanded form (vv. 6-7), for we hear what preceded the crisis. The suppliant had gotten into dangerous complacency and no longer realized that his prosperity depended entirely on God's goodness, which God could take away at any moment. Then came the catastrophe, and for the first time the suppliant really knew God, and cried to him from this trouble (vv. 8-10). His supplication is recorded in detail, underscoring for us the close connection of the IP to the IL psalm. In verse 10 we find the two parts of the petition; in verse 9 we find the reasons which should persuade God to hearken to the petition.

Verses 11-12. The account of the rescue can now be very brief, because almost everything it wishes to say has already been said. In one image of singular poetic beauty the effect of God's deed and the deed itself are simultaneously described:

Thou hast turned for me my mourning into dancing,
    thou hast loosed my sackcloth,
    and girded me with gladness. . . .

With a childlike directness that combines the external with the internal with radiant joy, here the psalmist unites the reversal of suffering in his own life with the activity of the eternal God. This bears testimony to the same God whom the ancient story in Genesis 3 says clothed the man and the woman as a sign of forgiveness.

Verse 12 is the expanded vow to praise. The psalm concludes with a promise by the person who is doing the praising that this praise of God in his or her life would remain alive. It is not as if the psalmist had completed a "thank you" to God, as we might express it; the confessing praise streams out into the expanse of time, into the expanse of existence which henceforth is to be marked by praise.

This conclusion of the psalm of narrative praise clearly points in the direction of descriptive praise. For the praise of God which will "not be silent," but which will fill the life of the person who has been rescued, does not need the special occasion of a specific deed by God. God can be praised in a comprehensive, general way which sees the manifold activity of God in all places—in the total fullness of God's being and activity. In Psalm 40 a statement is quoted by those who join in praise with the person who had been delivered (v. 16). They will say continually, "Great is the Lord!" That is a typical statement of descriptive praise. Also in Ps. 30:4-5 the summons to the surrounding circle of listeners to join in praise is based on a sentence of general praise of God (see above; likewise Pss. 116:5-6; 138:5-6).

The statements indicate that a living connection exists between the narrative praise of the individual who experienced salvation and the broad stream of the praise of God, which is not called forth by any special occasion. This praise is sounded forth, first and foremost, in worship. It is something which in all religions constitutes an essential part of the liturgy —*doxology* in its manifold forms. It is accompanied by sacred music; without it worship and sacred rites are unthinkable.

It is important to note that one source of this broad stream of doxology, of praise of God, and indeed perhaps *the* source, is confessing praise, which arises directly from the experience of a deed of God in the life of a person or of a community.

In conclusion, the surprising fact should be noted that in the IP psalms enemies never play the same role that they do in IL psalms. They are only mentioned (Ps. 30:1b). But in not even a single psalm of this group of psalms is the notion developed that the enemies have now been punished and how wonderful that is. Is this not a sign that for those who prayed these psalms, the act of God ultimately went far beyond opposition to the evildoers and their deeds?

5

The Psalm of Descriptive Praise
or Hymn (H)

The texts

This type includes Pss. 8; 19A; 29; 33; 57:7-11; 65; 66:1-7; 89:5-18; 100; 103; 104; (105); (107); 111; 113; 117; 134-136; 139; 145-150. In addition there are sentences or sections in all "liturgies" (cf. pp. 101-108 below), individual statements of praise in many other psalms and the concluding doxologies at the end of each book in the Psalter. This type also appears in Exodus 15, Isaiah 12, the doxologies in the book of Amos, Jeremiah 10:6-16, the praise of the seraphim (Isa. 6:3), and many other passages. Outside the Psalms the praise of God is most richly developed in the book of Deutero-Isaiah and the Book of Job. Also pertinent are the psalms in the Chronicler's History (1 and 2 Chronicles, Ezra, and Nehemiah), in the Apocrypha, and in the New Testament (esp. Luke 1:47-56 and Revelation).

The liturgical activity

The psalm of descriptive praise or hymn (Hebrew: *těhillāh*) is a uniquely liturgical song, the song of a congregation gathered for worship. Neither worship nor cultic celebration seems ever to have existed without songs which have praised the deity or deities. Hence this sort of song is found in most religions on earth, and the psalms of praise in Israel's neighborhood, especially the Babylonian psalms of praise, show many similarities to those of the Psalter. Psalms of this sort, hymns, were often accompanied by instrumental music of various types, as can be substantiated from the Psalter (e.g. Psalm 150). In fact songs of praise which celebrate God are one of the most important sources of music the world over. When in a church service today a congregation sings a song of praise to the accompaniment of an organ or of instruments, the same thing is happening that happened two and a half millenia ago in the temple at Jerusalem. But it is also the same thing which happened in worship many millenia before that in ancient, now-defunct cultures and religions all over the world—whenever a group of people gathered at a sanctuary to sing praises to their god.

If today some of the same Christian hymns of praise (esp. versions of the Psalms) are sung in both Protestant and Catholic churches alike, and if such hymns of praise and their melodies unite the church of many nations, all that is in keeping with the fact that all of the psalm genres it is this one in which we find the greatest affinity to the songs of praise in other religions. It is easily understandable that in the praise of God "at all times and in all places" much is held in common by all religions. In an ancient Babylonian prayer to Nanna (cf. ANET pp. 385-386, abridged) we hear,

Father Nanna, lord of Ur, hero of the gods,
Gracious Father, who hast taken the life of the entire land into
  thy hand,
Lord, thy divinity extends as far as the distant heavens and the
  wide sea, full of terror,
Thou, who hast created the land, founded the sanctuaries and
  hast called them by name,

Thou, Father, who hast begotten men and gods,
Thou who sittest upon a lofty throne and determinest sacrificial
    offerings,
Thou who callest kings, bestowing scepter and determining destiny
    for days to come. . . .

Just as in all religions the festive praise of God has its place
in the cultic assembly, so it was also in Israel. However, as in
all religions, the praise of God could not be restricted to a
single activity in a worship service. Because it was not prompted by any specific event (as was the case with an IP psalm),
this sort of descriptive praise could be raised whenever the
assembled congregation wished to honor its God: at the major
festivals, at sacrifices, and at worship services of all sorts. This
was true of worship taking place in the temple as well as (and
especially) at family celebrations of such events as the Pass-
over, the beginning of the Sabbath, and numerous other special
occasions.

The "Chronicler's History" (1 and 2 Chronicles, Ezra, Nehemiah) reflects the great significance of the Psalm of praise in
postexilic worship. The book of Tobit in the Apocrypha shows
how pious Jews scattered far and wide from their homeland,
nevertheless lived in the Psalms. By using the Psalms in their
homes and in their rooms, such diaspora Jews participated in
the worship of their people, a worship which could not be
restricted in time and place. It was in this way that the psalms
of praise, especially, moved from the worship of the temple
into the synagogues and then in the early Christian church.
From there, in turn, they moved into the houses and families in
many places, in many ages. Wherever a song of praise is raised,
there worship takes place, whether it is in a room where a
family gathers, in a cathedral, or in the cell of a prison.

An example: Psalm 113

Verses 1-3. The same sort of call to praise in the imperative which we found in the midst of the IP psalm as a call to the surrounding listeners to join the person who had been rescued in praising God (30:4) forms the introduction to most hymns. It is meant as a genuine summons, which presupposes that it is both necessary (since God's praise can disappear from the lips of an individual or of a community) and possible (because, even when God's praise becomes less strong and vocal, someone is always present to summon the rest to take it up again). Why the summons? Because the summoner has experienced the reality of God in an overwhelming manner. The many calls to praise God (which often fill an entire psalm) are not dead liturgical formulas; they are also not merely a kind of sonorous prelude to the psalms. Every one of these calls to praise God originated in some confrontation with the living God and is intended to carry the echo of that confrontation further.

Hence this call to praise God presses on throughout the entire Psalter to an even broader and indeed most distant horizon, to "not be silent" (30:12). In the introduction to Psalm 113 this desire to extend the praise of the Lord to the farthest possible extent is expressed in an especially clear and deliberate manner. The call to praise, directed to those who wish to serve God is extended in v. 2 "from this time forth and for evermore," in v. 3 "From the rising of the sun to its setting. . . ." The praise of God should extend to the uttermost limits of time and space, for only thus can God be affirmed as the Lord of time and space, no matter how far they may extend. These two verses also give us a hint of how we are to understand the fact that in the Psalms the (heathen) nations and their kings are also included in this call to praise. Yes, creation itself, animate and inanimate creatures, is summoned to praise God. This is possible because for the persons who sang these psalms God was so powerful that there dared be no limitation in acknowledging him.

Verses 4-9. The main part of the psalm gives the reason for this call to praise. Accordingly, the psalm of descriptive praise consists of only these two parts: (a) the call to praise and (b) the unfolding of that praise. Its structure might be viewed from the situation of a hiker who has discovered, as he was walking a bit apart from the path his group had taken, a marvelous view of the landscape. He calls the others to come and view it, and their joint viewing becomes an awestruck, marveling description of the view before them. One can elaborate this image. There are many possibilities for such a description. The decisive thing, however, is whether the description simply enumerates what is seen, without careful selection, one item after another, or whether in what is seen *one* single impression is so dominant that the entire description is derived from it and merely unfolds it. These two possibilities also present themselves for structuring the praise of God: (1) it can simply enumerate, one after another, all kinds of things about God and God's acts which are to be praised; but it can also (2) be so struck by one singular characteristic of God that this one attribute determines the descriptive praise down to the very details themselves. The second possibility is the one which is characteristic of the hymns of the Old Testament. Psalm 113 can best demonstrate that for us. If a person reads it often, it becomes clear that its main section, vv. 4-9, pivots on vv. 5 and 6, on the statements,

There is none like the Lord our God
    in heaven or on earth,
who sets his throne so high
    but deigns to look down so low . . . (vv. 5-6 NEB; the text as given in the RSV must be rearranged).

In these statements at the very heart of Psalm 113 we hear the astonished echo of a basic experience with God, an echo in which *all* has been gathered that can ever be said of God: This is our God, the majestically exalted one, who does not remain in this exalted state but looks far down into our depths. This is the God who heard the cries of the children of Israel in their slavery and came down to save them. This is the God of Hannah, Samuel's mother, who hearkened to her when she cried from the depth of her despair, and who graciously favored her. This is the God to whom those who pray Psalm 123 say, ". . . as the eyes of servants look to the hand of their master . . . so our eyes look to the Lord our God, till he have mercy upon us" (v. 2). This is the God whom the poet of Psalm 23 celebrated: "Even though I walk through the valley of the shadow of death, I fear no evil; for thou art with me . . ." (v. 4). It is not too much to say that the affirmation at the heart of Psalm 113 is the basic statement of the praise of God in the Psalms.

This basic statement concerning God's majesty and his mercy stands at the center of all of Israel's descriptive praise. If the Psalms wish to tell in summary fashion who God is (and this cannot be done in factual and objective statements, but only when one is caught up in praise), then in some way these two polar statements are there, two statements which belong together like two poles in one field of magnetic energy.

It is easy to recognize very clearly how this statement in Psalm 113 is central to the entire psalm. The one side, God's majesty, is elaborated in v. 4: God is highly exalted above all people (all nations) and above all creation (above the heavens). The other side of the central statement is elaborated in vv. 7-9: God looks far down into the depths. This means that God discovers there in the depths the trouble of those who suffer. And now this looking down into the depths must prompt another movement by God: drawing those in misery out of their darkness:

He raises the poor from the dust
  and lifts the needy from the ash heap (v. 7).

Verse 7 describes (anyone can easily see it) precisely what was declared by the persons who had been rescued in the IP genre, namely that God discovered them in their degradation and drew them up from the pit, from the underworld, from death. Likewise something we noticed before in discussing the call to praise is here corroborated: descriptive praise is derived from confessing or narrative praise and is closely connected with it. But now, in vv. 8 and 9, something new has been added. The psalms of narrative praise only looked back to the hour of rescue; the psalm of descriptive praise, however, goes beyond that and pictures the new life which is given to the one who has been rescued. Here also the difference between these two genres can be clearly seen. By means of two typical examples, the psalmist shows what was changed when God looked from the heights into the depth of human suffering. In both cases the suffering (as we find it again and again in the psalms of lament) was not just trouble in a material sense; it was also an event which happened in a social context. This suffering has its sting in the loneliness and shame into which it brings the sufferer. This side is the one in which is shown God's intervention which changes the course of events. The man who had been driven out of the circle of his clan's honorable men by his suffering is now restored to his former place in society; the barren woman who had become a social nonentity because she had no child, and therefore no status, is now restored to a place of honor in her home as the happy mother of children.

Thus the central statement of this type of praise (praise which celebrates the God who looks from the heights into our depths) extends from the majesty of the Lord high above the heavens to a little room in a house where a mother rejoices with her child. It extends from the festivity of a hymn sung at worship to everyday life in a village where the men sit together in the evening. But this broad scope only corresponds to the broad field of the central statement. Such is the God who is praised here.

The structure

The psalm of descriptive praise or hymn does not have a structure as clear-cut as the psalm of narrative praise. Nevertheless there is one basic structure which undergirds the very different sorts of psalms of this genre, the same structure we have identified in Psalm 113. It is this consistent structure which clearly distinguishes the Old Testament "hymn" from those of the Babylonians and Egyptians, hymns with which they otherwise have many things in common. The hymns of the Old Testament never consist only of a piling up of doxological attributes and of long chains of doxological statements. They are the unfolding of *one* basic polar statement which provides the undergirding for all psalms of this genre.

(a) The *introduction* is the call to praise. The call to praise, given in the imperative, is a unique characteristic of this genre. Only later did it enter other types of psalms (psalms of mixed genre). We have a good illustration of the fact that originally this was a genuine summons (not part of the psalm itself, but its prelude) in Neh. 9:5ff: "Then the Levites . . . said, 'Stand up and bless the Lord your God. . . .'" And then the psalm of praise followed. This was also a genuine summons in the IP psalms, in which the person who gave an account of his deliverance summoned his listeners to join in the praise (30:4; 34:3). At first this summons consisted of only one sentence with one verb: e.g. *Halělû Yâ* ("Praise Yahweh"). Then it was expanded with additional words describing the Lord, or the imperatives were changed to jussives (e.g. Ps. 113:2-3, "Let the name of the Lord be praised!"—literal translation). This element (the call to praise) grew more and more; it could be repeated again before the second part, and added again at the end (Psalms 100; 97) until there developed out of it an independent type of psalm which was entirely dominated by the imperative (95A; 145; 148; 150).

(b) The *main part* always includes the two sides of the praise of God which stand at the center of Psalm 113. They are often summarized in a sentence or two at the beginning of the main part:

> . . . his judgments are in all the earth.
> He is mindful of his covenant for ever . . . (105:7-8).

> Praise the Lord, for the Lord is good;
>   sing to his name, for he is gracious! (135:3)

> For I know that the Lord is great,
>   and that our Lord is above all gods (135:5).

> O give thanks to the God of gods,
>   for his steadfast love endures for ever!

> O give thanks to the Lord of lords,
>   for his steadfast love endures for ever! (136:2-3)

This double statement about God does not always have to stand so clearly and programmatically at the beginning; it can also be what stands hidden behind the structure of a hymn of descriptive praise. But it is always present. This can be noticed even in such a short psalm as 117 (probably once the concluding doxology of a small psalm collection). These two fundamental statements about God which control the psalm of this type are then unfolded in a balanced manner: God shows his lordship and majesty by being Creator and Lord of history; God shows his goodness and compassion by rescuing and preserving. This can be illustrated in the structure of two psalms:

	Psalm 33	Psalm 136
summons to praise	1-3	1-3
reason for praising: God's activity	4-5	1-4
as the Creator	6-9	5-9
and the Lord of history	10-12	10-22
as the Deliverer of his people	13-19	10-22
the Deliverer	18-19a	23-24
the Preserver	19b	25

The correspondence between the two psalms is not as precise as it might appear from a superficial glance at this outline, which is intended only to show how the unfolding of the two-fold statement concerning God's majesty and compassion controls both psalms. In Psalm 136 the two motifs "lord of history" and "deliverer of his people" coalesce in a presentation of the history of the people. In Psalm 33 the simple expression about the deliverance is varied: the eye of the Lord is not on the mighty but on those who fear him. But in both these psalms the other main motif ("deigns to look down so low") is most assuredly present (Pss. 33:14 and 136:23). Here we see that *one* theme is fundamental in the many variations. Praise of the Creator is found in Psalms 33:6-9; 65:6-8; 135:6-7; 136:5-9; 146:6; 147:4, 8, 16-18, and in many other places; the praise of the Lord of history appears in 33:10-12; 65:7; 135:8-12; 105:7ff; 146:3-5. How the composers of the Psalms sensed that both motifs belonged together is shown by a verse which brings both into a close unity:

. . . who dost still the roaring of the seas . . .
   the tumult of the peoples (65:7).

The same all-encompassing view of God's creating and history-controlling activity is expressed in a marvelous way in Deutero-Isaiah's proclamation, which in this instance is based on psalms of descriptive praise:

I made the earth,
  and created man upon it;
it was my hands that stretched out the heavens,
  and I commanded all their host.
I have aroused him (Cyrus) in righteousness,
  and I will make straight all his ways (Isa. 45:12-13).

The statement that God looks down from on high and has compassion on those in the depths is repeated in 113:5-6; 33:13; 136:23; 147:6; Song of the Three Young Men 1:32; Luke 1:48. God is praised as Deliverer in 65:2-3; 89:14-18; 135:14; 136:10-22; 146:7-9; 147:2-6; and often outside the Psalter until Luke 1:48, 50, 54-55 and 2:14b. Less frequently the praise of the Preserver is added to the praise of the Deliverer: 33:19b; 111:5; 136:25; 145:14-15.

Further developments. Hymns are not always controlled by the two basic statements of praise in the same manner and with the same emphasis. Sometimes the center of gravity shifts to individual points; sometimes such parts become independent psalms. In the book of Psalms itself that does not happen regularly; in the postcanonical psalms it happens much more often.

The full weight of Psalm 103 is centered on the praise of God's grace, but this psalm, too, ends in v. 19's praise of God's majesty, and the unfolding (as Creator and Lord of history) is sounded in vv. 7 and 14.

In other passages we can observe the way in which the praise of God's goodness becomes independent in the statement which gradually separates itself from its context: "O give thanks to the Lord, for he is good," which recurs like a litany throughout the entirety of Psalm 136 and is already found completely isolated in Ezra 3:11; 2 Chron. 5:13; 20:21; Jer. 33:11. Complete and exclusive praise of God's grace is found in Pss. Sol. 2:33-37; 5:1-2; 10:1-8; 18:1-5.

The basis for the manifold call to praise in Psalm 150 is solely God's majesty; this is likewise true in the concluding doxology of Pss. Sol. 18:10-12 (cf. also 1 Chron. 29:10-12).

6

Creation Psalms

An elaboration of the motif "praise of the Creator" resulted in independent psalms 8; 19A; 104; 139; (148); Amos 4:13; 5:8-9; 9:5-6; and many sections in Deutero-Isaiah and Job.

Psalm 8. This psalm begins and ends with praise of God's glory. The amazed observation of God's glory in creation soon turns from the vast horizon of the heavens to one point: human beings as God's creatures. When the psalmist's view turns from the vastness of the heavens to tiny human creatures, and in amazement asks, ". . . what is man that thou art mindful of him . . . ? (Ps. 8:4), then what again rings in our ears is the statement at the heart of Psalm 113. Even the babbling of a tiny infant bears witness to God's creative power and is thereby stronger than all the gainsaying of God's enemies (v. 2). God considers tiny beings as close to the divine, and shows this by letting them rule over the work of his hands—animals of all sorts. We moderns can hardly understand how lordship over the animals is a sign of honor bestowed upon us, for here we have an echo of a feeling for life from a very ancient age, an age for which the domestication of animals was humanity's highest achievement.

Nevertheless we moderns can repeat this psalm's praise of God in its essential lines also today. Think how much greater the gap between the vastness of cosmic space and our smallness on this tiny planet has become! Think how our lordship over creation has grown! How mighty God would be for us in our world, as God was for the psalmist's world, if we could but simply marvel and be amazed at these new perspectives we have gained and if we could but look from them to the Creator!

Psalm 19. Like Psalm 8, this psalm starts with praise of God's majesty, something which the heavens are telling. The first verses of this psalm do not describe what in Christian dogmatics is called "natural revelation." Such an approach misunderstands the psalm completely. The heavens declare the glory of God, not in order to reveal God, but in order to exalt, praise, and laud the God whose existence and activity is presupposed as the most real of realities. Something like a revelation of God or knowledge of God from nature would be senseless and utterly absurd in the Old Testament. Much better would be the opposite approach: God was so real and so powerful to the people of the Old Testament and to the people who prayed these psalms that creation also must have been conceived of as participating in exalting and praising God's glory. Precisely in this respect the sun of this Psalm 19 is something completely different from matter. It has been drawn into what constitutes the meaning of *all* that has been created, the praise of God.

In our time the creation psalms again receive important significance, because in the light of science and its results, as well as in our present stance toward nature, the deification of nature has no future (not even if it were to come in the most subtle form of Idealism). There remain only two alternatives: materialism or faith in the Creator. Either the stars, the atoms, and the earth are only matter—then we human beings must be understood as coming from matter and consisting of matter—

or else the stars, sun, and earth are related to God just as we are; they are creatures. In that case the ultimate meaning of their existence is the same as that of humans: existing to the praise of God's glory.

Psalm 104. Here again we find in the introduction of the psalm the praise of God's greatness: "O Lord, my God, thou art very great; thou art clothed with honor and majesty." This, then, quickly goes over to a description of creation. But almost without our noticing, in place of a description of the creation of the world at the beginning we hear of God's creative activity at the present time. A lively, radiant picture arises before our eyes. The praise of the Creator becomes a description of nature: a description, however, which again and again always returns to its origin: "O Lord, how manifold are thy works! In wisdom hast thou made them all; the earth is full of thy goodness" (v. 24).

Psalm 104 is so similar to an Egyptian hymn, Akhenaton's "Hymn to the Sun," that a connection or dependence upon it is often assumed. This is entirely possible, because in the description of creation a point of contact with other religions is entirely understandable and meaningful. All contemplation and description of nature in the whole world once grew from praise of the Creator. All feeling for the beauty of nature has its source in the creature's remembrance of the common origin of all that is created.

The praise of the Lord of history did not lead to such a fixed group of psalms. Nevertheless, just as in creation psalms the motif "praise of the Creator" became independent, similarly the other motif of psalms of descriptive praise, "praise of the Lord of history," was gradually expanded and finally became an independent entity. It is possible to observe with some clarity that gradual filling out of this motif in the Psalms. In Psalm 33:10ff we hear only that God topples the mighty but grants his chosen people salvation. In Psalm 135:8-12 this is expanded: God smote Israel's foes in Egypt and Canaan and gave the Promised Land to his people. The report in 136:10-22 is still more extensive, beginning with the smiting of the first-born in Egypt and ending with the gift of the Promised Land to Israel. Finally, in Psalm 105 and Exodus 15, this motif from the Psalms became dominant.

Alongside this development occurred another. "The praise of the Lord of history" was combined with a feature which was customary in prophecy, a reference to the earlier sins of the fathers, their punishment by the Lord, and the repentant return of those who had been punished. Such speaking of history, which is ultimately always aimed at the instruction and admonition of contemporaries, appears in various compositions of mixed genre: it combined with forms of wisdom speech (Psalm 78; Deuteronomy 32); it penetrated the community laments (Psalm 106; Isa. 63-64; cf. Nehemiah 9); and, last but not least, it is met in the genre of psalms of descriptive praise (Pss. 81:6-16; 95:8-11; cf. 99:5-9).

7

Liturgical Psalms

Those psalms are called *liturgies* which are clearly shaped by some liturgical activity, those in which a combination of liturgical speech with liturgical action can be recognized. In its simplest form this might consist only of clearly recognizable antiphonal dialog. Such antiphonal dialog at worship always presupposes, as far as we know, an activity (stylized as it may be): an interchange between two groups, or between a liturgist and a congregation—summons and response to a summons. In addition there may be actions such as prostration, bowing, rising, movement of the hands, walking in procession, entering the sanctuary area, walking around the altar, performance of an act of dedication, of a sacrifice, of a sacred meal, etc. A good example of such activity is found in Deuteronomy 26, which describes how a farmer who brings the firstfruits to the sanctuary, recites a creed along with the giving of his offering.

The Psalter does not contain many psalms of this nature. No psalm reproduces a complete worship service. The liturgical action is always merely alluded to. For the Psalter is not an order of service; it does not contain rubrics which tell what

actions or movements are to be made at specific points. The
Psalter is more like one of our hymnbooks than a minister's edition of our orders of service. It is meant for the congregation
and therefore contains only the words to be prayed or spoken
by the congregation. So liturgical actions are only alluded to.

Sacrifice of praise and psalm of praise

Psalm 66. In explaining the IP psalms we made reference
to the connection between a sacrifice of praise and a psalm of
praise (both are called *tôdāh*). Surprisingly enough, in only
one of the psalms of this type is the sacrifice expressly named:
Psalm 66. Verses 13-15 of this psalm reproduce the declaration
of sacrifice, i.e. the words which were spoken at an actual
offering of a sacrifice. This declaration of sacrifice is clearly a
liturgical statement of what must be done. If it is reproduced
only this one time in connection with its proper psalm, but is
missing in all the other psalms of this genre, this is a sure sign
that the Psalter has transmitted songs to us as songs already
separated from sacrificial action. However, we can assume
that originally a sacrifice was connected with every such
votive psalm and that a declaration of sacrifice was part of
a sacrifice.

Besides this brief liturgical formula in Psalm 66, the Psalter
contains two liturgies which show that the individual's psalm
of thanksgiving had varied significance for worship: 118
and 107.

Psalm 118. In this psalm all reference to the sacrifice of
praise is missing; in its place is the narrative praise of an individual (vv. 2-7, 17-20) combined with a procession, during
which the gates of the temple were entered (vv. 19-20) to the
accompaniment of snatches of antiphonal dialog reminiscent
of Psalm 24. Part of the procession was a festive dance in which
the altar was encircled, branches in hand (v. 27). From inside
the temple a blessing was pronounced by the priests upon this

procession (26-27a). This is not all crystal clear, and individual expressions can be understood in other ways. But what is certain is that the psalm represents a festive observance by the congregation and that a psalm of narrative praise stands in its center. Verses 22-25 are apparently the congregation's answer to a rescued person's narration about God's act.

Psalm 107. This is a psalm of descriptive praise, consisting of a combination of four songs of confessing praise by four persons who had been rescued. A traveler who lost his way, a prisoner, a sick person, and a sailor who had met danger at sea—all four bring their confession of praise into the presence of God at the sanctuary. Their experiences of deliverance are summarized each time in a refrain which occurs at the end of each of the four accounts:

Let them thank the Lord for his steadfast love,
  for his wonderful works to the sons of men!

The psalm begins with the call to praise (v. 1) and ends with praise describing God's rule (vv. 33-43). This highlights what is taken over in our hymn: "True wonders still by him are wrought, who setteth up and brings to naught" (*TLH* 518). What is especially characteristic of the praise of God in the Psalms is this personal experience by individuals, personal experience which is gathered together in joint praise of God. These individuals learned to understand that what they had experienced was God's doing, and they must now give testimony of it before the congregation. In the great traditional intercessory prayer of the church petitions are made for those at sea, for travelers, for the sick, and for prisoners. As in Psalm 107, these also have their place in the worship of the church. The question, however, remains whether we perhaps should not engage in "intercessory praise" corresponding to our "intercessory petitions" as is done here in Psalm 107.

Pilgrimage songs

The very journey to a sanctuary was itself considered part of the sacred activity by people of earlier ages. It was part of what had to be observed. Hence the pilgrimage song in its original sense was not simply a song sung on the way to a sanctuary, but rather the words belonged to this observance. In it was expressed what was going on in the pilgrimage, and that meant above all the departure from home and the arrival at the sanctuary. These two key points of the journey are the two foci about which the pilgrimage song revolves. Traces and imitations of pilgrimage songs are frequent in the Old Testament, but the Psalter contains only one real pilgrimage song, Psalm 122.

Psalms 120-134 all have the superscription "pilgrimage song" (this translation is not entirely certain). To be sure, this small collection contains only one true pilgrimage song, Psalm 122. It is likely that the concept was later generalized (as in our pietistic designation "a pilgrim's song"). Yet on this basis we can most certainly assume that collections of pilgrimage songs once existed, to which all sorts of other songs were later added. In the western world pilgrimage songs became the most important sources for traveler's songs; and it is still possible to recognize that many early German traveler's songs had their origin in pilgrimage songs.

Psalm 122. This psalm has a very simple structure. The first two verses speak of departure and arrival:

I was glad when they said to me,
    'Let us go to the house of the Lord!'
And now our feet stand within your gates, O Jerusalem!

Verses 3-5 are an expanded address directed to Jerusalem, which at the same time gives the reasons for making the pilgrimage. Verses 6-9 greet the city in the form of a wish that it may be blessed.

The pilgrimage song is imitated in Isaiah 2:3 and Micah 4:2; Jeremiah 31:6; Isaiah 30:29; there are reminiscences of it in Genesis 35:3; Psalm 132:7. Psalm 84 is a further development, the greeting to Jerusalem having become the main part. In Psalm 87 the greeting to Jerusalem is central, but its derivation from a pilgrimage song is hardly recognizable. Similarly in Psalm 48 the greeting of the city has become a song praising the city of God. The last two psalms, however, already belong to a different group: the songs of Zion.

Songs of Zion

Songs of Zion are found in Psalms 46; 48; 76; 84; 87. This group is most likely related to pilgrimage songs, but their essential content is no longer the journey to Zion or the wish of blessing for Zion. Rather they focus on the city of God's preservation from enemy attack. In the background of these psalms stands the tradition which claimed that Zion, with its temple and city, had been chosen as God's mountain. Before the city gates occurs a great battle against the Gentiles, in which the Lord remains the Victor, entering the city in triumph. This victory of God on behalf of his city is observed with a procession (48:12-13). Psalm 46:9 apparently also refers to this procession. Psalm 76 (vv. 3-6) looks back at the battle and celebrates the Lord's choice of Zion (v. 2). But it seems at the same time to look forward to a coming victory of the Lord over the nations when he comes to hold judgment (vv. 8ff.); then all the rest of the nations will acknowledge him (v. 10). The same motif occupies an important place in the enthronement psalms.

Psalms of blessing

Just as the journey to the sanctuary (the journey itself and the arrival there) was important, similarly also the journey from it (the departure from the holy place) was so important that it appears in the Psalms as a distinct feature. When they left, those who had come to the sanctuary received a blessing which was indispensable for daily living. All important celebrations at the sanctuary ended with the bestowal and reception of the blessing. It is to be expected that this also is reflected in the Psalms.

In the above-mentioned liturgy, Psalm 118, the blessing is alluded to: after the congregation's petition (v. 25) the priests spoke the words of blessing (v. 26):

Blessed be he who enters in the name of the Lord!
  We bless you from the house of the Lord.

We have an almost identical benediction at the end of Psalm 129 and a similar one in 134:3.

Psalm 121. This is a genuine and specific psalm of blessing. The first verse summarizes in very stylized form the turning of one who is seeking help toward the sanctuary; the second expresses the confidence of the one who needs help that he or she will be heard. From vv. 3-8 a different voice speaks: a priest speaks a blessing to the one leaving the sanctuary. Besides the general blessing which the congregation as a whole received, there must have existed also a special assurance of blessing for the individual, such as is preserved in Psalms 121 and 91. The address which is directed to an individual in both psalms can hardly be understood otherwise than as a direct, personal assurance, which was given to an individual in the temple in response to a prayer and confession of trust (91:2; 121:2; this is also mentioned in Ps. 128:4-5). The same combination of confession of trust and assurance of blessing is found in Ps. 115:9-15, though in this case it is directed more to the entire congregation. Also in the procession psalm, Psalm 24, the goal is reception of the blessing (v. 5). Psalm 67 contains a petition for blessing as well as actual reception of the blessing, combined with a summons directed to the nations to praise God.

It is striking that nowhere in the entire book of Psalms is blessing spoken of so much as in the small collection of pilgrimage songs, Psalms 120-134. This seems to show that an essential goal or the chief goal of a pilgrimage in Israel was to receive the blessing. It also indicates most clearly that at one time many more words of blessing and psalms of blessing existed than have been transmitted to us in the Psalter. Psalms of blessing like 91 and 121 are liturgies in the genuine sense of the word: they include both antiphonal speaking and action.

Entrance instructions

Several psalms permit us to see that on specific occasions entrance into the sanctuary and reception of the Lord's blessing there were limited by prerequisites. In Psalm 24:3 worshipers arriving at the entrance to the temple precinct put the question,

Who shall ascend the hill of the Lord?
    And who shall stand in his holy place? (v. 3)

In verses 4-6 they receive an answer (coming from the direction of the temple, undoubtedly from a priest). It states the conditions for entrance into the sanctuary area: "He who has clean hands and a pure heart. . . ." Psalm 15 is such an entrance torah or instruction. In answer to a question it gives information about the prerequisites for entrance into the sanctuary. Verse 1 puts the question; vv. 2-5 give the answer, which in this psalm is more detailed than in Psalm 24. The same sort of entrance instruction occurs again in Isaiah 33:14-16, and, in

varied form, in Micah 6:6-8. The context in which these entrance instructions stand has been illumined by the study of
comparative religions; many religions had something similar.
A unique further development is represented by the Egyptian
Books of the Dead, in which entrance instructions have their
place at the entrance into the land of the dead.

Procession with the ark

The second part of Psalm 24 most likely presupposes a procession with the ark. Verses 7-10 are antiphonal dialog. A group
arriving either at the fortifications which crowned Jerusalem's
acropolis on Mt. Zion or at the temple demanded that the
gates be opened for the king (v. 7). Those within asked the
question who this king might be. The group outside responded
with a doxology of this King (v. 8). The same dialog is repeated. It is generally assumed that this song was chanted
antiphonally between two choirs at the moment when the ark,
carried in procession, arrived at the gates which guarded the
temple precinct. Whether Psalm 132 also belongs to a procession with the ark can no longer be asserted with certainty. At
the very least a reference to such a procession with the ark can
be recognized in the way in which the passage through the
Jordan River is described in Joshua 3 and 4.

There certainly must have been many such processions in
ancient Israel. About all we hear concerning them, however,
are occasional general references or allusions. The action and
the accompanying words have not been preserved and transmitted in the book of Psalms. Psalm 24 is a sample of many
similar texts which accompanied liturgical action; but in what
has survived for us it is a rare exception.

8

Royal Psalms

Royal psalms are found in Psalms 2; 18; 20; 21; 45; 72; (89); 101; 110; 132 144:1-11. Royal psalms are those in which the king plays a role. They do not represent a special genre of psalms; they and the various situations presented in them are too diverse for that. Kingship arose in Israel only comparatively late; hence kings never played such a dominant role in Israel's worship as they did in neighboring empires. Therefore the royal cult did not shape any special genre which might be called the royal psalm genre. What we term royal psalms are to a large extent psalms of hybrid or mixed genre, i.e. those in which one of the other psalm genres can still be recognized.

Nevertheless it seems that in the days of Israel's preexilic monarchy many more royal psalms existed, i.e. psalms in which the king played a special role. Even those royal psalms which have been preserved in the book of Psalms were at one time most certainly related to the living kings of Israel and Judah. For instance, intercessions were prayed in behalf of the contemporary reigning king. Most of these royal psalms, however, were incorporated in the Psalter as the book developed in postexilic times, because these psalms were interpreted with a view to the long-awaited king of the future. Their original meaning, i.e. their relation to the currently reigning king, is therefore often difficult to recover. In the meaning which was subsequently given to them they bear witness to messianic expectations in the worship of the postexilic congregation.

Psalms 2 and 110. These psalms were apparently connected with the celebration of the king's enthronement. In *Psalm 2* a divine oracle for the king (vv. 4-9) is sent forth into the midst of a situation fraught with threats for the people (vv. 1-3). The oracle for the king promises him victory over his enemies. In this connection the king is designated God's son; v. 7 is an adoption formula. Psalm 110 is similar. However, it consists only of the divine oracle directed to the king. Here also the king is placed in very close proximity to God: "Sit at my right hand . . ." (v. 1). Moreover, the king is confirmed in his office by God. These two psalms became important for the Christian church in its messianic interpretation of them because what was here spoken of an earthly king was transferred to the Messiah as God's Son, sitting at the right hand of God. Insofar as these psalms in a later time were an expression of hope in the coming Messiah, this transfer is justified. But it should also be noted that if they are related to the historical kings of Israel— and that is how they were originally intended—their effect is rather strange in their relation to the Psalms as a whole. Elsewhere in Israel's worship kings were never referred to in such lofty terms. Also, except for Psalm 110, the rest of the Old Testament does not speak of the kings of Judah as possessing any priestly office. Also striking in this connection is the precise designation "after the order of Melchizedek" (v. 4), i.e. according to the manner of the pre-Israelite, Canaanite king-priests of Jerusalem. Some scholars have supposed that in the background of this psalm stands an ancient, pre-Israelite ritual. Similarly it is possible that Psalm 2 had an origin in pre-Israelite Canaan. In any case these psalms do not reflect the specifically Israelite, specifically Old Testament conception of kingship. This is found rather in Nathan's promise (2 Samuel 7) on which all of **Psalm 89** is based.

Psalm 132. This psalm reflects a special liturgical celebration of the Lord's choice of both Mt. Zion and the dynasty of David. It contains (v. 17) also the expectation of a coming king. **Psalm 45** is a wedding song for a king, sung by a singer at the royal wedding. A literarily beautiful song, it describes for us the wedding celebration of an Israelite king in brilliant, clear colors. But it is really a completely secular song, which originally had nothing to do with worship. It got into the Psalter only because it was subsequently interpreted as referring to the Messiah, the end-time king, and thus became an expression of the expectation of this future king who was to come.

Intercession for the king occupied an important place in Israel's worship. **Psalm 72** is totally an intercessory petition for the king, as is the beginning of **Psalm 20** (between 20:1-6 and 7ff a divine oracle for the king is to be assumed) and the beginning of Psalm 132. In 61:7-9 and 63:12 the intercession for the king appears as an appendix.

In recent decades the royal psalms and their relation to the royal cult in Israel have been the subject of much careful research and many scholars have engaged in far-reaching speculations, on the assumption that the king was the chief personage in Israel's worship. Not only the royal psalms, but also the entire genre of individuals' psalms of lament, were understood as royal psalms. This, however, is extremely questionable and even the few truly royal psalms say nothing about a cult led by the king in Jerusalem.

9

Enthronement Psalms

Enthronement psalms are found in Psalms 47; 93; 96-99. The introductory shout in many of these psalms, "The Lord reigns" or "The Lord is king," has been interpreted by Mowinckel as "The Lord has become king." He set up the hypothesis that from the times of the early monarchy Israel celebrated, in connection with the autumn new year's festival, a festival of the Lord's enthronement. At first his hypothesis was accepted rather widely. It certainly represented some sort of breakthrough and had the stimulating effect of prompting the appearance of many studies which sought to relate specific psalms to specific festivals. More recently, however, Mowinckel's hypothesis has been challenged at a number of points.

Psalms 93; 97; 99 all have the introductory shout "Yahweh is (or has become) king!" In **Psalm 93** this shout is followed by the praise of his majesty (vv. 1-2), an account of Yahweh's victory over hostile forces (vv. 3-4), and praise of the law and of the temple (v. 5). In **Psalm 97** the introductory shout passes over into a description of God's epiphany (vv. 3-5); following this are words of praise, which exalt God over the gods, and an exhortation to hear God's voice (vv. 6-12). In **Psalm 99** the introductory call is likewise expanded by praise of God (vv. 1b-4), whereupon a small section, complete in itself, follows (vv. 5-9) in which elements of descriptive praise are combined with elements of instruction from history. **Psalms 96 and 98** are psalms of descriptive praise, expanded by the motif of the royal reign of God and the announcement of God's advent as Judge of the world (96:13; 98:9). **Psalm 47** alone alludes to the inauguration of the royal reign of God. In this case, then, we can most easily imagine a liturgical rite, perhaps even a procession.

A common feature of all these psalms (in addition to the cultic cry, "The Lord has become king" found in all but Ps. 98) is that God is praised for his majesty, with special emphasis put on the reign of Israel's God over the entire world: 47:1-2, 7-9; 96:1-3, 7-10, 13; 97:1, 5-7, 9; 98:9; 99:1-3. Beyond that, Psalms 96 and 98 announce God's coming to judge the nations of the world. Both themes belong together, for the worldwide rule of Israel's God can only be the long-expected coming rule of God. The liturgical and eschatological interpretations of these psalms are not mutually exclusive. Borrowing the customs and imagery of the enthronement of an earthly ruler, the community celebrated in these psalms the future inauguration of God's royal rule over the entire world, anticipating the fulfillment of the promise in liturgical jubilation.

10

Wisdom Psalms

These psalms present us with a unique type of literature, somewhat transitional between worship psalms and instruction in wisdom. In wisdom literature we distinguish between the wisdom saying and the wisdom poem or song. Both these types have connections with the Psalms. In the small collection of pilgrimage songs, Psalms 120-134, we find a few wisdom sayings which by themselves have no relationship or connection with worship psalms (127:1-2; 127:3-5; 133). These are three proverbs that deal with ordinary daily life. The first contrasts human strivings and God's quiet rule. The second celebrates a large and healthy family. The third does something similar except that in this case it is presented as the reward for fearing God (thus also in 128:1-3). These three "psalms" could appear in the book of Proverbs without changing a word, and no one would imagine that they were supposed to be psalms. These proverbs in the heart of the Psalter show that in the late period psalms and wisdom (to be specific, wisdom that had become theological) had come to be closely related.

Psalm 37. The same thing holds true in a different way in the case of proverbs which have been combined with a psalm, as is the case especially with Psalm 37. Here we have a different group of proverbs which deal with the righteous and the wicked, contrasting the two groups, calling for the fear of God, and warning against evil and foolishness. In this theme of the opposition between the righteous and the wicked, the Psalms and the wisdom literature of the later period come into contact with each other. Psalm 37 is, as a whole, the instruction of a wise person, who warns hearers against being upset because of the wicked (vv. 1-2, 7b-8; cf. 49:16), but exhorts them to trust God (vv. 3, 5, 7, 34, 37), for God will finally punish the wicked and grant salvation to the righteous. Without any change this entire psalm could also be a chapter in the book of Proverbs; it has entered that completely into sapiental speech. The fact that it was included in the Psalms shows again how flexible the boundary between the Psalms and wisdom had become in the late period. Then a sort of devotional, pious poetry was current, one in which the prayers of the Psalms came into contact with something entirely different, namely wisdom. Yet unlike the earlier group (Psalms 127 and 133), Psalm 37 shows affinity to a specific genre of psalms, the IL type. Behind the coolness of the admonitions addressed to righteous persons can be felt the hidden heat of passionate pleading such as we met in this genre's complaints about enemies. When the wise person admonishes, "fret not yourself over him who prospers in his way" (vv. 7-8), this amounts to a pleading question, "How can you, O God, permit such a thing?" The description of the wicked is identical with that in the IL psalms, and as is the case in expanded psalms of lament, we hear of the final destiny of the wicked and, by contrast, the righteous (vv. 17-20). Thus it is understandable that psalms and wisdom come into contact at this point.

Precisely this contrast between the righteous and the wicked fostered the appearance of a special group of psalms: 1; 112;

and 128. The same contrast also appears in a whole series of individual passages. **Psalm 1.** This psalm has been placed at the beginning of the Psalter as a prologue, something which assumes the late understanding of the Psalter just described (as a book of pious edification). It contrasts the two "ways," that of the righteous and of the wicked (v. 6), and congratulates the righteous person on being truly fortunate (vv. 1-3) in contrast to the evildoer (vv. 4-5). The contrast is expressed in a metaphor which is applicable not only to the late age in which Psalm 1 was affixed to the book of Psalms but to the Bible in general, to show what a person is like who is with God or without God: like a tree planted by streams of water or like chaff which the wind drives away.

Psalm 112. This psalm is like Psalm 1, as is also Jer. 17:5-8 (almost verbatim). The contrast of the two ways is a frequent motif in late Judaism. A close parallel to Psalm 1 is Psalms of Solomon 14.

Congratulation of the pious person as truly fortunate also occurs a number of times in other psalms (41:1-2; 84:12; 119:1-2). It grows directly out of praise of the person who has been rescued in Pss. 34:8 and 40:4, "Blessed is the man who makes the Lord his trust."

Psalm 49. The contrast between the rightous and the wicked was not always so clearly marked as in the above-mentioned group of psalms. The vexations and temptations to despair which the good fortune of the wicked produced in the righteous, and which could not be completely hidden behind the wise admonitions of Psalm 37, are also reflected in a number of psalms which are lament psalms in genre but which represent the transition from lament to meditative reflection and then to wisdom speech. Typical of this group is Psalm 49. Like a wisdom poem, the psalm begins with a detailed summons to hear (vv. 1-4). What follows is expressly described as "wisdom": "My mouth shall speak wisdom" (v. 3). But then, rather abruptly, the question is put:

Why should I fear in times of trouble,
    when the iniquity of my persecutors surrounds me,
men who trust in their wealth
    and boast of the abundance of their riches? (vv. 6-7)

The question about the good fortune of the wicked is answered with reference to their fate in death (7-11, 13-14). Finally, in sharp contrast, the person who had raised the question at the beginning experienced the certainty, "But God will ransom my soul from the power of Sheol" (v. 15). With this "but," this wisdom psalm gives evidence of its origins in the lament. Its "but" marks the turning point from the complaint to the certainty of having been heard.

The element of reflection appears in the exhortations (Pss. 49:16; 94:8-13) and especially in the reference to human transitoriness, a reference which leads from complaint to meditative reflection. In Psalm 39, which likewise begins with the perplexity caused by the godless (vv. 1-3), this is especially prominent (vv. 4-6, 11).

Surely every man stands as a mere breath!
    Surely man goes about as a shadow!
Surely for nought are they in turmoil;
    man heaps up, and knows not who will gather! (vv. 5-7)

This motif is developed in a magnificent manner in Job 7 and 9-10.

Psalm 73. This psalm begins with the same problem raised in Psalms 49 and 39, ". . . I saw the prosperity of the wicked." This is unfolded so vividly in vv. 4-12 that we can appreciate the weight of the vexation and temptation to despair. The psalmist grants that in view of the prosperity of the wicked he had almost stumbled (v. 2), and his complaint describes in classic manner what we today call despair. What almost brought the psalmist to a denial of God was not, as is usually the case of the psalms of lament, the fact of being endangered or hard-pressed by evildoers (as e.g. in Psalm 22), nor yet the suffering which he had to endure (the I-complaint). Rather, it was being vexed and tempted to despair by evildoers' continuing success and prosperity, while the righteous suffered in an impotent, senseless manner.

But then comes the turning point: ". . . until I went into the sanctuary of God" (v. 17). Here we see that, despite its reflective character, Psalm 73 is a genuine psalm with roots deep in worship. But in place of an oracle of salvation, the gift for which suppliants came to the sanctuary, in this psalm what has tipped the scales and effected the reversal is the fact that God's hitherto hidden activity is now perceived, understood, and acknowledged. The one who prays recognizes that the evildoers had been delivered to ruin and vanity (vv. 17-20); but he, in contrast, could be completely certain of God, even in the face of death (vv. 23-26). The concluding contrast in the fate of the wicked and of the righteous (v. 28) comes back full circle to v. 1:

Truly God is good to the upright. . . .

Other genres of psalms also permit us to recognize the transition to wisdom speech that took place. This is very clear in the case of individuals' psalms of praise. In **Psalm 34** the person who had been delivered called on the bystanders to join in praising God (v. 3). To this is attached (in typical wisdom style) an exhortation to trust (v. 5), which is continued in vv. 8-10 with a promise for the righteous. In vv. 11-14 we hear the same summons to listen which we found in 49:1ff (similarly also 51:13):

Come, O Sons, listen to me,
  I will teach you the fear of the Lord! (v. 11)

Attached to this is an exhortation to the pious life. The praise of God with which the psalm concludes (15-22) is interwoven with the contrast in the fate of the righteous and of the wicked. Psalm 92 concludes in a very similar manner (vv. 9-15), its portrayal of the righteous reminding us of Psalm 1. The beginning of this psalm also reveals points of contact with wisdom speech.

Among the psalms of descriptive praise, **Psalm 111** is usually considered a wisdom psalm. But it is to a greater degree a pure psalm of praise in which the two main parts are clearly discernible: praise of God's majesty (vv. 2-3, 9c, 10c) and of God's goodness (vv. 4-9). Only at the conclusion is a wisdom saying added to the psalm, the same proverb which we find in Proverbs 1:7. Similarly, at the conclusion of Psalm 107 stands an exhortation addressed to wise persons. It bids them to heed what has been said.

Of all the psalms of praise in the book of Psalms, **Psalm 139** is the one which is most strongly reflective, but it is still, even with these reflections, entirely praise of God. In the post-canonical history of psalms of praise, however, sapiential speech and the didactic manner of speaking become ever more prominent, as is seen in Sirach 39; 42 and Psalms of Solomon 3.

11

Psalm 119

Psalm 119 is often also considered a wisdom psalm. But what it contains is not really wisdom speech but a great doxology of God's word, of the law of God as it is called most often in this psalm. We have said that this psalm is devotional poetry and not a psalm in the genuine sense of the word. It was composed to edify (in the good sense of that word). Almost all psalm types and psalm forms occur in it, but they have been fitted together in a manner that is far removed from the living, organic totality of real psalms. Each new group of eight lines begins in the original Hebrew with the same letter of the alphabet; that pattern continues through the entire alphabet.

If a person succeeds in reading this psalm's 176 verses one after the other at one sitting, the effect is overwhelming. In its extent the psalm has the effect of a massive mountain range. One has the feeling that it represents the boundary between the world of the Psalms and a different world, that of law piety. The authentic and genuine nature of this latter dominant motif is not to be doubted. Here a person bears witness to the fact that God's words (no matter how understood) have become the foundation and content of his life. Authentic existence, meaningful life is seen as possible only through devoted attention to these words:

Teach me, O Lord, the way of thy statutes;
　　and I will keep it to the end (v. 33).

This person knows that without these words he could not really find his way in the world, in life, or in life's problems:

Thy word is a lamp to my feet
　　and a light to my path (v. 105).

But we note that already here "the law" has become a uniquely independent entity which often almost takes the place of God:

If thy law had not been my delight,
　　I should have perished in my affliction (v. 92).

Still stronger are the statements in vv. 48 ("I revere thy commandments") and 50. Here a profound change is beginning: God's word is now no longer the word which confronts a person directly to comfort, instruct, judge, or warn, but is an existing entity, the written Word of God transmitted as scripture, at the center of which stands the Law. In Psalm 119 this religion of law sends out from a distance, as it were, an announcement of its eventual arrival on the scene. The word of God is still a living entity for the person who prayed this psalm, as is apparent from the amazement which grips the psalmist as he stands before the profound and incomprehensible mysteries of this word:

Open my eyes, that I may behold wondrous things
　　out of thy law (v. 18).

12

Conclusion: Psalm 90

We put Psalm 103, with its praise of God's goodness, at the beginning of our study. At the heart of Psalm 90, by contrast stands the statement,

... we are consumed by thy anger;
  by thy wrath we are overwhelmed (v. 7).

Psalm 90 belongs to the genre of community laments, but nothing of the structure of these psalms remains except the petition,

Return, O Lord! How long?
  Have pity on thy servants! ...
Make us glad as many days as thou hast afflicted us,
  and as many years as we have seen evil (vv. 13, 15).

In this petition we recognize once again the two elements of the petition as well as vestiges of the complaint. But it is only in these last verses that it becomes clear that the psalm is really a lament or a petition of the people. The entire middle part (vv. 3-12) is the unfolding of a motif which does not really belong to this genre and which we otherwise find only as an expansion in IL psalms (esp. 39 and 49). We found this allusion to human frailty also in Psalm 103 (vv. 14-16), and in point of fact there it was set, as in Psalm 90, in contrast to God's eternity.

If a community psalm of lament is so strongly marked by the proclamation of human transitoriness, and if the reign of God's wrath is seen to be responsible for the frailty of human life in a manner that brooks no reservation, then we are hearing in Psalm 90 the voice of a later age, an age for which God's wrath has become a dark and burdensome reality. Von Rad has rightly placed this psalm as a neighbor of the book of Ecclesiastes and has drawn attention to the fact that in this psalm the history of salvation has been silenced almost completely. This is something which was more or less part of the whole in community laments, as God's past aid was reviewed. On the basis of the same experience Israel's wisdom in one of its branches found its way into the closest proximity to skepticism. The burden of a history in which God seemingly no longer helped his people for centuries at a stretch was a burden too heavy to bear. Nothing of God's goodness was any longer apparent and therefore these people pleaded with God,

Let thy work be manifest to thy servants,
and thy glorious power to their children (v. 16).

But just for that reason the first statement of this psalm becomes all the more significant:

Lord, thou hast been our dwelling place in all generations.

At least this one statement at the beginning reminds us that God had been the refuge of his people generation after generation (cf. Ps. 22:3-5). And it is only from the perspective of this introduction that all of Psalm 90 can really be understood. Even if the late generation which expressed its experience of reality in this psalm was far, far removed from the deeds which God once did for the salvation of his people, even if it also had to see, without making any reservations, that its own reality was characterized by complete transitoriness in the presence of God—

For we are consumed by thy anger . . ." (v. 7)—

the fact that this view of reality was *still brought before God,* the fact that people who could no longer recognize anything of God's activity or of his glory in their world *nevertheless pleaded* with this angry God who was hidden to them—that fact is based *only* on one thing, namely that these people still stood in the chain of a tradition in which it was told from generation to generation that God could be depended on.

If the contrast in this psalm were only between the *thought* of human transitoriness and the *thought* of God's eternity, then these thoughts also would be part of the grass which soon withers. But what is crucial in Psalm 90 is the *fact* that people with an extremely sober recognition of the transitory nature of human existence (a recognition that bordered on skepticism) called, in the midst of these facts of their own history, on the God who in his anger and wrath stood behind these realities. They continued to plead, "Turn again, O Lord, unto us." The venturesomeness of this pleading with the God of wrath, however, was based on the connection which, despite everything, still remained intact, and which this later generation still possessed: the connection with the fathers and their praise of God.

Thus Psalm 90, with its affirmation of God at the uttermost limits of existence and its extreme restraint, is very far removed from the exuberant praise of God's goodness in Psalm 103; but both "musical modes" heard together make up the genuine tonality of the Psalter. Psalm 90, with its plea for reversal at the verge of death, stretches out toward a deed of God which might finally make God's works and glory visible once again. This is one of the statements on the edge of the Old Testament which calls for something entirely new.

Finally, in the contrast of Psalms 103 and 90, what was set forth at the beginning as characteristic of the Psalms should again be clear: the polarity of lament and praise that corresponds to the polarity of the anger and mercy of God. The cry to God in the Psalms lives from the fact that the God who sits enthroned high in the heavens looks down into the depths:

Lord, thou hast been our dwelling place in all generations.
Before the mountains were brought forth
    or ever thou hadst formed the earth and the world,
    from everlasting to everlasting thou art God (vv. 1-2).

13

The Psalms and Christ

In three passages the Psalms point unambiguously to what has happened in Christ. They do not point to it by way of "prophecy," as that word was previously understood. Such prophecies (in the sense of predictions, which later generations found in single statements of the Old Testament detached from their context) cannot be the basis for the relation of the Old Testament Bible to the New Testament Bible. The Christ event is anchored in the Old Testament in a more profound and comprehensive manner.

1. We found at the center of descriptive praise the statement in Psalm 113,

There is none like the Lord our God,
 in heaven or on earth,
who sets his throne on high
 but deigns to look down so low (vv. 5-6 NEB).

Here, as we said, confessing praise has been transformed into a description, a declaration. This is the God to whom those who prayed the Psalms (individuals as well as the total community) cried—and this is the God who helped them. This is the God who is praised by the confession of those who have been liberated, the individual as well as the community. This same statement points beyond itself directly toward Christ, toward God's act of sending his Son. God's looking down from the heights into our depths became a definitive event in the coming down of his Son. In him the gracious Word of the Father took on flesh and blood; he "emptied himself, taking the form of a servant . . . " (Phil. 2:7). What is called "condescension" in Christian dogmatics and the basic message in the hymns sung at the celebration of Christ's birth ("He who Himself all things did make/A servant's form vouchsafed to take/ That he as man mankind might win/And save His creatures from their sin" *TLH* 104) is all, in a genuine and full sense, the fulfillment of the heart of Israel's descriptive praise of God. Hence it is not accidental that this motif from the Psalms extends directly into the New Testament in the prologue of Luke's gospel; in the song of Mary (Luke 1:46-55) and of Zechariah (Luke 1:67-79):

. . . through the tender mercy of our God,
when the day shall dawn upon us from on high
to give light to those who sit in darkness and in the shadow
    of death (Luke 1:78-79).

2. Those "who sit in darkness and in the shadow of death" are those whose laments constitute a great part of the Psalter. If God's looking down from the heights into our depths became reality in Christ, then God's coming down into "our poor flesh and blood" also means that God became one who suffered, and that this suffering was expressed in lamentation. The New Testament expresses this clearly by incorporating Psalm 22 in the passion story. The frequent quotations from this psalm in the passion narrative indicate that the primitive church saw a connection at this point. Above all, Mark 15:34, Jesus' cry from the cross that uses the initial words of Psalm 22, indicates how the primitive church saw this connection. It understood that

Christ made the lament of Psalm 22 his own lament. How much Jesus himself must have lived in the Psalms! How much the first Christian community must have lived in the Psalms if it was Psalm 22 in particular which became *the* psalm of the passion story! In this psalm the depth of the lamenter's vexation and temptation to despair and the miracle of the reversal of his suffering come to unique expression. By taking into himself this last trial of being forsaken by God, Christ descended into the depth of human isolation and made our suffering his suffering to its depths. The despairing questions of those who suffer in our world (Why? How long?) are questions which were known by him in whom God's goodness became human. They are not foreign to him. He took our suffering as part of his suffering to the fullest possible extent. Psalm 22, however, was taken up into the passion story as a representative of psalms of lament in general. All of them come to their goal in the suffering and death of Jesus Christ. How the lament itself changes because of this was shown in our section concerning the enemies in psalms of lament: complaints about enemies no longer have to lead to petitions directed against these enemies. Into the place formerly occupied by petitions against enemies comes, as the passion story indicates, intercession *for* them.

3. If, however, Psalm 22 was incorporated into the passion story, then such incorporation must include the entire psalm. For viewed in its totality, Psalm 22 is a lament which has been reversed. Its second part (from v. 22 on) is praise by a person who has been delivered, praise which has anticipated the actual deliverance. Just as it can be said in the second part of Psalm 22,

For he has not despised or abhorred
   the affliction of the afflicted;
and he has not hid his face from him,
   but has heard, when he cried to him ... (v. 24).

so, similarly, the proclamation of the earliest messengers of the resurrection was full of the message that God responded to the cry from the cross. The message of Easter is narrative praise. It is possible that the phrase that appears in Matthew's Easter account, "go and tell my brethren" (Matt. 28:10) is an allusion to the beginning of the second part of Psalm 22, "I will tell of thy name to my brethren." Whether or not this is a quotation from Psalm 22 is unimportant. What *is* essential, however, is the fact that the statement at the center of the resurrection message, "whom God raised . . ." has the structure of narrative praise, "God has acted!" The examples of the first sermons of the apostles show how this ultimate deed of God was viewed, as the last in the succession of God's great deeds, which in the Old Testament had aroused praise from the liberated. In this connection it is possible to see a consistent feature in the individual's psalms of praise, that those who there praised God understood their deliverance as being snatched from death. Likewise the statements of confidence in Psalms 16, 73 and elsewhere express the conviction, " . . . thou dost not give me up to Sheol . . . " (16:102).

The apostles, as messengers of Christ's resurrection, stand in the succession of witnesses to the great deeds of God. They are witnesses who, in the Psalms, must give an account before the whole congregation about what God had done for them. Now that the time is fulfilled, the call to praise God, which had its origin in this witness to God's deeds, is the call to follow Christ. As in the Psalms nations and kings were called to join Israel in praising God, so the call now has transformed itself into the message of Christ's messengers, who carry the call to come to Christ farther and farther, even to the ends of the earth.

From the rising of the sun to its setting
  the name of the Lord is to be praised! (Ps. 113:3)

Select Bibliography
Works in English for Further Study

Introductory

Clements, Ronald E. *One Hundred Years of Old Testament Interpretation.* "Interpreting the Psalms," pp. 76-98. Philadelphia: Westminster, 1976.

Gunkel, Hermann. *The Psalms: A Form-Critical Introduction.* Philadelphia: Fortress, 1967. (fundamental; with an introduction by J. Muilenberg and bibliography)

Westermann, Claus. "Psalms, The Book of." *The Interpreter's Dictionary of the Bible.* Suppl. vol. Nashville: Abingdon, 1976.

Commentaries

Eaton, John H. *Psalms.* Torch Bible Commentaries. Naperville: Allenson, 1967. (popular, but reliable)

Toombs, L. E. "The Psalms." *The Interpreter's One Volume Commentary on the Bible.* Nashville: Abingdon, 1971. (introduction and notes for the general student)

Weiser, Artur. *The Psalms: A Commentary.* Old Testament Library. Philadelphia: Westminster, 1962. (an all-around commentary)

Special Studies

Eaton, John H. *Kingship and the Psalms.* Studies in Biblical Theology. Series 2, no. 32. Naperville: Allenson, 1976.

Guthrie, Harvey H. *Israel's Sacred Songs: A Study of Dominant Themes.* New York: Seabury, 1966.

Mowinckel, Sigmund. *The Psalms in Israel's Worship.* 2 vols. Nashville: Abingdon, 1962. (the cultic background of the Psalms)

Shepherd, Massey H. Jr. *The Psalms in Christian Worship: A Practical Guide*. Minneapolis: Augsburg, 1976.

Westermann, Claus. *The Praise of God in the Psalms*. Richmond: John Knox, 1965. Out of print. (a study of the categories or genres of the Psalms)

Westermann, Claus. *Praise and Lament in the Psalms*. Atlanta: John Knox, 1981. A reprint of the above title with additional material on the psalms of lament.

Westermann, Claus. *What Does the Old Testament Say About God?* "The Response," pp. 65-80. Atlanta: John Knox, 1979. (outline of the theology of the Psalms)

Westermann, Claus. *The Old Testament and Jesus Christ*. "The Response of God's People and Jesus Christ," pp. 61-68. Minneapolis: Augsburg, 1970.

Westermann, Claus. "The Role of the Lament in the Theology of the Old Testament." *Interpretation* 28 (January, 1974) :20-38.